Mother Mary Francis, PCC
Feb. 14,1921..Feb.11,2006

Forth and Abroad

Mother Mary Francis, P.C.C.

Forth and Abroad

Still Merry on Land and by Sea

A Sequel to
A Right to Be Merry

Ignatius Press   San Francisco

Cover illustration by Sister Mary Pius, P.C.C.
Cover design by Riz Boncan Marsella

© 1997 Ignatius Press, San Francisco
ISBN 0-89870-589-4
Library of Congress catalogue number 96-83639
Printed in the United States of America ∞

To my eighteen thousand sisters—
the Poor Clare Nuns
spread over the world

Contents

Preface

Once upon a time there was a little book called *A Right to Be Merry*. It was written because we needed, urgently, to repair our enthusiastically leaking roof and had no money to accomplish that. Our founding abbess, Mother Immaculata, saw an ad in a Catholic paper: "$1,000.00 prize for a first book by an unknown author." Realizing that I was highly qualified by reason of never having written a book and being thoroughly unknown, Mother told me to "write a book". Obedience simplifies all things. So, there was no room for questioning and even less for objecting. It remained only to inquire what the book should be about. "I don't care", replied Mother Immaculata, giving this yet further evidence of her broad, sweeping vision and knowledge of how to delegate work. However she added, if not ominously at least definitively: "But win the prize. We have to get the roof repaired."

That made my plan of procedure clear. So, I rummaged about in the piles of old, used Christmas cards people had given us, flattened them out (cards, not donors), and wrote the story of our Poor Clare life on the backs of the cards. Choosing the subject of the book posed no problem. It was only a clear matter of writing about what I love with all my heart: our blessed vocation, our way of life. On old Christmas cards, and in oddments of time here and there, it was written. We never entered the contest because Frank Sheed, dinner guest at the home of a professor-friend of ours at Notre Dame University, picked up the few type-script chapters I'd sent to said friend and asked to publish them and the chapters to come, sight un-seen.

So many, in the ensuing years, have asked for a sequel to *A Right to Be Merry*. This is it. Sequels are oftentimes quite deadly. We hope this one is not. One ecumenical council and five foundations later, we're still merry.

Chapter I

First Summoning

"What does she see?" I inquired of myself. I did not inquire directly of Sister Anthony, whose unswerving gaze at a point on the ceiling of her little infirmary cell was intriguing me, because she was too busy. Sister Anthony was dying, and she was giving to this present task the same focused attention she had given to every other charge and detail of her sixty years of Poor Clare living. She seemed clearly to be already in another world where we could not follow her. Intent, unblinking, she lay there. And I, perched on a high stool beside her bed, sat there. One just does not ask questions at such a moment in such a situation. But then the young novice mistress, her little flock of novices and postulants fluttering about her, came in.

It was time for the changing of the love-guard that kept watch beside Sister Anthony all the days and nights of those final weeks of her last November in Roswell. And our hope-for-the-future contingent very much wanted to know what Sister Anthony was seeing at that point above her which so compelled her gaze. Having none of the inhibiting hesitations of their abbess, they sought clear explanations, no matter the hour or the situation. "Do you see our Blessed Mother, Sister Anthony?" the self-appointed spokesman wanted to know, probably hoping against hope for an affirmative answer sure to elicit a whole litany of subsequent inquiries. It was a dramatic moment as Sister Anthony slowly turned her gaze away from its upward intentedness to the little hopefuls around her. She studied her young questioner with something that made me think of the Last Judgment. I could only reflect within myself that dying Sister Anthony looked strikingly like living Sister Anthony had always looked: businesslike, no-nonsense, practical, and conclusive. The eager question still hung upon the air: "Do you see our Blessed Mother?" "No, dear Sister", replied Sister Anthony in a tone that left no doubt as to her opinion about seeking after the phenomenal. It was, in fact, the briefest and perhaps most effective instruction I have ever had regarding the perils of desiring visions and all such. After this devastating negative, Sister Anthony returned to her study of the ceiling.

Then, on November 28, 1969, having just attained her eighty-first year, Sister Anthony departed to initiate our first foundation, a foundation assuredly destined to endure by reason of its being made in eternity. And it was an especially fitting time, since the Roswell foundation was just come of age, it being twenty-one years precisely that November since eight of us had come to put down our Poor Clare roots in an old white farmhouse just outside the city limits of Roswell. We had come by God's grace to number thirty this historic November, but we still held fast to our conviction that foundresses scarcely ever remain upon this earth long enough to be part of yet another foundation. This one newly made by Sister Anthony in eternity would, we could be certain, grow. And even as we sorely missed her unique earthly presence, we could without doubt anticipate each of us returning to her company to enlarge Roswell's foundation in eternity during the unfolding years. No one, of course, had any intention of going anywhere else. "Eternal rest grant to her, O Lord", we besought that Lord for our Sister Anthony. Only, she did not rest. Things began happening.

Less than two years after the summoning voice of God had spoken his "Forth and abroad!" to our first vicaress in Roswell, he was to sound that call to five of us for Roswell's first foundation in the vestibule of eternity, that is to say, upon earth. Sister Anthony had always wanted to get things done on earth right away. It seemed evident that she was continuing this mode and manner in the celestial realm. It was likewise manifest that God endorsed this plan of action and had, as a matter of observable fact, initiated it from the beginning. That is, he again made himself quite and painfully clear.

There was a vacated monastery in a southern State, and there was a wonderful bishop who did not wish it to remain such. "Will you come?" he asked us. In the kindest and gentlest manner, the good bishop yet made it discomfitingly clear that if Poor Clare life was not to be any longer in his diocese, it would obviously be our fault. If the Lord Jesus was obliged to fold his tabernacle-tent and take his Eucharistic departure, the responsibility for such a heartrending exodus would be ours. There followed, after a short measure of time allowed us to emerge from initial shock, a series of community discussions. It was just early post-Vatican II, and collegiality was the watchword of the hour. We were very collegial, each sister contributing her light on the situation and her considered opinion. The fact that all the lights were one light and all the opinions the same would doubtless be considered deplorable in any age of enlightenment, much less the somewhat panting atmosphere of the early seventies. But there was just no gain-saying it: we all produced one and the same scenario as we had this thing out with God. It could have been set down in script like this:

BISHOP: This monastery must needs be re-peopled.
ROSWELL COMMUNITY: Assuredly. We shall pray for that.
BISHOP: But you are the ones who must do it.
ROSWELL COMMUNITY: *We?* Oh, no. We do not want to go anywhere. We like it here. We like each other. We shall never part from one another.
BISHOP: A tabernacle of the living God will be no more. No more adoration there.
ROSWELL COMMUNITY: Oh, so sad. We shall pray about it.
BISHOP: It's up to you to *do* something about it.
ROSWELL COMMUNITY (*Silence. Uncomfortable shifting about. Then, full chorus*): We do not want to go anywhere.
    Enter: The Presence of God, right.

Delighted in the sense of that Presence, the sisters articulate again their views about a new foundation with the unsurmountable obstacle of such an enterprise requiring some of them to be parted from the others of them, a possibility obviously not within their consideration. With happy certainty of divine endorsement, the nuns outline their position:

SPOKESMAN: We never want to leave one another. (*All are certain that God is pleased.*)

SECOND SPOKESMAN (*encouraged by the anticipated re-action to the community stance, speaks out firmly, certain of further divine approval*): We like it here. (*Gathering force*) We will never leave here.

All relax, in shared surety of God's approval. It seems time for a psalm, hymn, or motet expression of joyous satisfaction. Organist moves to exit on left to get the score. Is stopped. Everyone is stopped. Voice of God speaks clearly in each one's heart:

No community should ever make a foundation if any of its members are eager to get away from the other members. (*Uneasy silence as the sisters recognize their eligibility.*) No foundation will be firmly built except on the tears of those who wish never to be parted. (*Stricken silence as the sisters realize that in this they are well qualified.*)

THIRD SPOKESMAN (*with diminishing aplomb*): About that tent of yours in the south, God, we are terribly sorry to see it folded; but we know you understand. We can't . . . (*fidgets nervously*). So sad, but we could never leave one another . . . (*voice trails off under God's silent gaze*).

And in the heart of the community sounds the unmistakable summons:

Forth and abroad!

There is this about the "Forth and abroad!" that God sounds in dramatic high intensity and unmistakable clarity at certain times and in varying climes of the lives of his own: such summons are only the exceptional expressions of his low-murmured and unexceptional summons of each day. That primeval "Forth and abroad!" that sounded for each of us was actually completely inaudible save in the ear of the summoning God as he called us into being. This initial calling forth in our lives was heard only by Father, Son, and Holy Spirit. All the profound and interior summonings of our being to a fuller and truer expression of itself are equally soundless save in the inmost chambers of that being.

At the hour of human birth ordained by God, the time itself sounds the summons to come forth from the womb into the full light of earthly existence. It is a dramatic call at an electric hour to be matched only by the final earthly summons to go forth and abroad from time into eternity.

But in the secret chambers of the essenced spirit of each of us, there are daily and sometimes even hourly those spousal summonings of God to the soul. And it is these and more precisely our responses to them that determine the caliber of our lives. There is a "Forth and abroad!" from the daily blueprints of holiness we have designed for ourselves, the invitation to the invisible martyrdom of the heart in hidden ways we could not have dreamed.

"Come apart with me", spoken in the inmost recesses of the soul, is of itself indeed an appealing summons uttered by God to the soul. But the "apart" is often enough a parting from all that reason argues as viable or predicts as being fruitful, much less humanly inviting. The silent nudging of grace at the soul is a clarion in eternity but soundless upon the earth save in the recesses of the spirit.

It is necessary that we learn to recognize the "Forth and abroad!" of grace that summons us out of mediocrity into the reality of our destiny. It points to formidable oceans for the spirit to cross. It speaks the new language of grace. And one learns this language only by the full listening powers of the soul. Perhaps the most indisputable sign of vibrant life in and with Christ is the increasing ability to hear the low murmur by which he calls his beloved "Forth and abroad!" out of herself, her plans, her ambitions, her hopes, into the caverns of his incredible designs where only the language of total giving is spoken.

On April 24, 1971, the first contingent of Roswell foundresses took off. The second segment set out just after celebrating in Roswell on January 24, 1972, the eightieth birthday of Roswell's foundress. We do not ordinarily celebrate birthdays, not that we consider there is anything uncontemplative about having a birthday, and particularly not in an assembly where each one is decidedly happy that all the others were born. It is just that with celebrating anniversaries of Investitures and Professions, fêting folks on their namedays, and being in general kept very busy in the effort to pace out the liturgy's continual unfolding of celebrations, we find our festival schedule already carrying a full load. But, then, when the eightieth birthday arrives with its wondrous message of achievement, we reverse our custom and declare high festival. It was a fragilely beautiful octogenarian Mother Foundress Immaculata who sped off five young foundresses.

She evidently experienced, for all her tears mingled with everyone else's tears, a sense of achievement. Apparently zeal for the spread of God's Poor Clare kingdom moved her foundress' heart to be yet again herself a foundress. For, the next month she died. She went off to see how things were going with Sister Anthony's new foundation in eternity.

How do Poor Clares die? How does the mystery

of community reveal itself anew in the eternal birth that is earthly death? What is that mystery of community during life? And why is it a mystery?

There are perhaps no folk on the earth who live more closely than cloistered contemplative nuns. Day after day and night upon night, year in and year out, they are together. Together in the choir in the great chanted chorus of the Divine Office by day and by night and in the silent prayer of the gathered-together. In the daily works of their hands and their hearts. In the refectory at meals always taken together, in tilling the small soil of the monastery grounds together. Yet doing, rejoicing, suffering all things together, cloistered nuns are and remain notably individual. Each is her own expression in life of that idea of God's which is the charism entrusted to St. Francis, handed on by him to St. Clare, and delivered by her to each of her presently eighteen thousand daughters the world over, to the many thousands who have gone before and the many thousands more we can hopefully anticipate will come after. And each one in her death is significantly her individual self. If the first vicaress in Roswell died as her own dear, inimitable self, the earthly demise of Roswell's founding abbess was as classic as a Greek drama.

Mother Immaculata had been failing physically for some two years, her characteristic gentleness

opening like a ripening flower. Having given so
many permissions over so many years as abbess, she
later asked permissions with the grace and beauty
that long-nurtured obedience will invariably beget.
And so, that February morning when a young sister
came with the message that our Mother Foundress
was not feeling well and asked permission to lie
down, I remained some moments marveling at the
blessedness of humility, so lovely to behold, so en-
chanting to hear. "Yes, yes," I said, "of course."
But then a discomfiting intuition began to arise
in my heart. Is this different from the predictable
summons of her weariness? I went to investigate.
And as I bent over Mother Immaculata, she vindicated my intuition. She had an explanation to
make. "Mother, I am dying", she announced. My
own heart briefly ceased its beating as I gathered her
into my arms. There followed the most beautiful
Drama of Dying we could ever have desired for our
Mother Foundress. Our Franciscan chaplain again
gave Mother the Sacrament of the Anointing, as
she leaned back in her invalid's chair, and gave her
the Holy Eucharist as well. Then she just tilted her
head to the side and drifted into eternity. All was
peace.

We prayed the prayers for the dying. Father remained to lead the rosary and then to officiate,
there in Mother's little cell, as hebdomadary for

the Offices of Sext and None. Each sister came and knelt to kiss our foundress' lovely hand, a tender procession of loving homage to a valiant religious woman who had been faithful to the end. We read the Passion according to St. John, as was read at the dying of St. Francis and of St. Clare. We sang the Transitus of St. Clare, marveling, each in her own heart, at the appropriateness of the dying words of our Order's Foundress for the dying of our monastery's foundress: "Go forth in peace, my blessed soul. He who created you and sanctified you has loved you as a mother loves her child. . . . O Lord, may you be blessed for having created me!" We watched the alabaster hands that had built and toiled and consoled and been folded in prayer for more than sixty-two years in the cloister resting like dove-wings on her lap. We saw the dear face that had sagged with suffering all these past months regain the strong and noble outlines of her years of vigorous service. By six o'clock she was lying in state in the center of our cloister choir, the Paschal candle burning at her head, a flower in her hand along with the parchment scroll of her vows kept so faithfully for sixty years.

The funeral Mass was like a *marche triomphale*. Eight Franciscan Fathers celebrated her final earthly Eucharist. And Mother Immaculata, lying on her simple board planed and polished by her daughters, wearing the religious habit she had loved without surcease during life, with which she was robed in death and which she carried gloriously into heaven, a linen cloth embroidered by her daughters with the simple and greatest Word, and her last word on earth: "Jesus!" thrown over her feet, a circlet of fresh flowers on her head, was indeed a bride.

At the burial vault, we sang her favorite prayer to Our Lady of Guadalupe, the grand finale of the operetta version of Our Lady's story: "Make love burn brightly in our hearts all days . . . until you bring us safely to the vision of your most holy Son." A breeze rippled her veil as she lay there, God using nature as messenger to tell us that she lives more vibrantly than ever among us because now the love that burned so brightly in her heart through so many years has found new and eternal flame in the vision of that most holy Son of the Virgin Mary to which she has safely come.

And then, following upon the glorious entrance of number two foundress into our celestial foundation, I betook me to investigate how things were going in number one earthly foundation.

The particular domestic significance of new beginnings produces ineradicable marks upon its unfolding history. We began our new foundation by making ourselves a golden stairway. This concerned scraping off paint from the stair risers and repainting them with happy yellow paint that the interested sunlight recognized as having kinship with itself and consequently spotlighted with its own beams each day. Painting walls is one thing. Painting the risers of an angled staircase is another. One becomes expert in specialized athletic maneuvers, an expertise not unaccompanied by a protest of certain muscles not hitherto recognized as one's own physical property and an angularity of joints insistent on maintaining itself long after the cessation of the task that had engendered it. Take it from me as from one who knows. But it was to bear into our unfolding foundation history a prime significance: a golden staircase, always brightly beckoning us to come up higher into the mystery of our contemplative life, ever making ascent a beautiful thing.

Beginning a new foundation is always an educating adventure. The former community had generously left us their expansive library. Our desire to resituate this center of learning on the second floor developed into so major an operation that no one ambitioned to be recognized as the one who had conceived this idea. Nor was anyone so insensitive as to make any reference to the known fact that the idea had been my own. Doggedly, we carried boxes and boxes and boxes of books up the golden stairway that gleamed our fatigue into happy purpose. The dismantled metal shelves that had stood so modestly in the original library now revealed themselves as ready to reach into the next county when spread out flat upon the floor. It was one of those operations, mounting temptation whispered, that should never have been begun.

Clearly something had to be done to bring into a realizable goal these miles of dark green metal shelves and this Library of Congress assemblage of books spread out before us. So, we did it. We painted away the gloomy green in favor of a happy amber. And the whole spectacle was transformed, beginning with the spectators-in-action.

There were certain operations, though, that even our brightest energies had to recognize as beyond us. Like carrying a piano from the second floor down the angled stairway to the first floor unloading platform for things destined to move on and out. In this, feminine rather than feminist, we recognized anew the need for the male of the species. Four stalwart Irishmen rose to the occasion. And groaned with it. And staggered under it. At the landing platform, I surveyed our perspiring Galahads with notable pangs of conscience over having entrusted to ordinary mortal men what pertained to professional movers. I looked at the quartet speculatively. Had I opened the way to semi-invalidism for them? They mistook what lay behind this nervous appraisal. "She's changed her mind", said one. "She wants us to take it back upstairs." One just cannot travel a golden stairway without coming to an agility of mirth. Or to an ever-deepening understanding of the divine mirth of cloistered living.

St. Clare traversed narrow stairways at San Damiano in Assisi, that first Poor Clare foundation ever. And she made them golden by her traversing. "*Vade, secura*", she encouraged her own soul when on her deathbed. "Walk on securely."

If St. Clare in her dying could calmly, almost gaily, direct her soul to go on walking forward, it was only because she had kept on walking forward all her earthly life. Her famous word to her daughters that they "walk with light step and unstumbling feet" is truly a lovely word. It is also a stern call to faith, the kind of faith particularly needed in answering the call to go forth and abroad on a new foundation. Whether to walk on with unstumbling feet pertains to the pilgrimage of the spirit or the journeying forth to a new monastic beginning, there are always things to make us stumble. The path is not an easy one down which we can lightly dance without any difficulty, not a smooth one on which we skip happily and unperturbedly along, but one on which we must walk. Walk. The word of the pilgrim. The essentially pilgrim person is always walking, and on a true pilgrimage it is a matter of hard walking.

There is not lush grass spread out before us but perhaps just a clump of grass here and there, some of it brown, much of it straggly and stumpy to scratch at our feet. There are the rocks of seeming unreality that must be on the pilgrim way. There are the little pebbles of frustration sometimes more difficult to deal with than the rocks. There are the brambles in the darkness of faith that we must go through and that prevent us from glibly calling ourselves contemplatives and women of faith while being without the suffering of faith. Spiritually there will always be the temptation to sit down and conclude that "it is too hard", to insist that everything must be made more pleasant. In the case of a new foundation, it is the sometimes insistent voice of the lagging heart: "Let's go back home." But there is also another voice in the heart, that of Christ, who says: "Forth and abroad!" And so we walked on in our new beginning, building happy living in the heart and in the house, too.

We had come into a very large monastery with a very small laundry. And God had sent us for our first birthday year of our first foundation two bonny postulants, showing in this, too, his preference for variation and a full assortment in a cloistered community. For one postulant gave clear evidence of being thoroughly Irish, and the other rendered ready proof of being as thoroughly Italian. We were growing. The laundry had to keep pace. No problem, we thought, as we explained to the contractor that the laundry needed to throw out its chest, and soon, as he could certainly observe for himself. But the man initiated us into a whole new world of committees and commissions and investigations and permits, a complexus happily unknown in the mothering monastery, where if one wished to hitch a new addition on to the old farmhouse, one simply proceeded with the hitching, no questions asked. Or answered.

Having learned much of the simple approach to happy living from the golden staircase, I bethought me to share this lore with the contractor. It was a brief scenario which I yet hold dear. It ran thus:

MOTHER MARY FRANCIS: Look, this is very simple. Just knock down the laundry's back wall. Then move the side walls out. Put a roof over the now roofless parts and close the whole thing up with a new back wall.

CONTRACTOR (*a large-sized Irishman*): Oh, Mother, you are a darling! (*embraces M.M.F.*).
Curtain

It needed only a year to enlarge the laundry. It required many years to enlarge the crowded choir.

And yet that, too, on its greater scale, was simple. We just knocked down the solid wall that separated cloister choir from public chapel (this with the help of architects, contractors, artists, masons, and assorted others) and raised up an open grille separation, a green-leafed iron affair with its gold-tipped leaves springing in a huge vine from the near life-sized image of the crucified Christ. Remaining unseen by the outside worshippers, we could now gather those worshippers in the chapel into the joyous cloistered chorus of our songs at Mass and our Office chants, our vigorous rosaries and all the rest.

Into this year of foundation God brought a foundation stone of our whole future life, though we could not have realized it at the time. Superiors representative of the different cloistered contemplative Orders were called to meet the newly appointed Secretary of the Sacred Congregation for Religious (as it was then titled) making his first trip to the United States in that capacity. Walking into the assembly room, I had my first glimpse of Archbishop Augustine Mayer, O.S.B. And I had a startling experience. Looking at this prelate from Rome whom I had never before seen either *in persona* or pictured, I thought: "But I know this person. I have *always* known him." What did that mean, that interior voice? I was to find out. We were all to find out. And we were to remember that it was in the year of our first going forth and abroad that God brought Archbishop (later Cardinal) Mayer into our lives.

Thus, the seemingly impossible unfolds, sometimes in laughter, sometimes in tears, and all made not just possible but imperative because God has spoken again: "Forth and abroad!" Now there was a confirmed new tenting place for the Eucharistic Lord of our lives. We had made our first foundation. And, assuredly, our last. So we thought.

Chapter II

Up North

In 1975, the diocese that enfolded our first foundation was divided, since it clearly provided a stretch
of land and need for episcopal care beyond the
reach of one bishop. A new diocese was created,
and its first and founding bishop installed.

He had much to look after in his newly assigned
borders, and he did. However, he also found time
to look around and eye a new community of Poor
Clares. He was greatly encouraged in this visual
exercise by his chancellor, a good friend and mentor of our first foundation. Episcopal optic considerations quickly developed into an idea. A large
idea that, when presented to us, at first engendered
none of the emotional churnings of 1971–72.

What was clearly called for and thus obviously a
call to which we should reply, explained the earnest
new bishop, was that we found another monastery,

this one in his new diocese. But, knowing this to be utterly impossible (another foundation after only five years!), we smiled our gratitude for the invitation and fell readily into total agreement that this new bishop was assuredly a man of God to be much admired for his spirituality, which urged him to establish without delay a cloister of contemplative nuns. It was, though, and of course, out of the question. We were completely comfortable in our clear understanding of this. Only there came again that Presence. That gaze, that voice in the heart. And the voice said so unmistakably: "Forth and abroad!"

To make definitively sure that we had heard the voice and recognized the Speaker, the new bishop and his new chancellor appeared at our monastery in December 1976, like two cedars of Lebanon, strong, sturdy, and sure.

"You have many sisters", pointed out the bishop. "But they are so young", I countered weakly. "I know many religious superiors who would love to have that problem", sweetly said and smiled the bishop. And it came to be that I had to confess aloud at our next community chapter that, while one is always free to say: "No!" and to bring forth the clear factual evidences that crowd forward in a dazed mind and a splintering heart, still one cannot deny that the voice of God has spoken in the soul. In March 1977, Sister Therese and I set out to select the site for our second foundation.

The weather at our arrival was just ideal for site-seeing. Sister Aloysia had arranged for that. At eighty-eight, tiny Sister Aloysia was obviously increasing in eagerness to be sent on to our foundation in eternity, although she continued her daily activities with purpose and dispatch. These included running a private laundry service for her own needs. Afflicted with eczema on both hands, her personal laundry equipment included an assortment of gallon cans, formerly the domiciles of coffee, applesauce, or tomatoes but now elevated to a higher cans-level as minor laundry sinks, and also the pink rubber gloves always worn to conceal from her eczema-ed hands the presence of soap water. In these famous cans were washed thoroughly and with notable frequency the various small cleaning cloths that pertained to the household shrine she maintained in the dormitory and the handkerchiefs she sentenced to unending extracurricular lavabos.

She was a dear and familiar sight on her daily and nocturnal journeys from dormitory cell to laundry and its outlying acres, for Sister Aloysia had already scorned the boundaries of earthly hours and was often enough inspired to initiate a new day's laundry service before cock-crow. Only the journeyings were made at an increasingly slower pace. Her private orisons, on the other hand, were increasing in pace and in volume.

Sister Aloysia was completely deaf in the final years of her precious life on earth. She attributed her non-hearing to the fact that the other sisters did not properly articulate their words, making it clear, by that time-proven pedagogical device of frequent reiterations of a basic premise, that if the sisters would speak clearly, she would hear them perfectly. "You don't articulate", she would point out to a sister, kindly but firmly, even as the sister in question was increasing her lung power to past-capacity with heroic effort and widely audible results.

Always a woman of firm decision, it appeared to Sister Aloysia, who had long since taken the abbess as her private charge in regard to matters of health, giving me frequent admonitions to "stay away from doctors" and to "eat a lot of chocolate" (the latter happy piece of advice being a health measure not at all easily attainable in the cloister), that the Mother Abbess should definitely not set out at February's end for a far-off State of the Union. How was she to prevent the departure? Well, there was one reason that would most certainly decide the abbess against setting out from Roswell at that time, and Sister Aloysia had recourse to it. She died.

We did not know that morning when our sister had to be taken by ambulance to the hospital that she would return only for her funeral, but we did know and forever afterward would appreciate that she left in her own inimitable high style, waving to the gathered community through the window where she lay in the ambulance, smiling as one who has ascended her chariot to ride off in glory. No more were we to hear her oft-repeated acclamation "Blessed be the holy name of Mary!" spiralling down from her dormitory cell and resounding with declarative emphasis to the community as we were gathered in silent prayer in the choir below. With the privilege of the totally deaf, Sister Aloysia prayed that favorite aspiration with full volume unheard by herself.

There was something of the *allegro-jubiloso* about her funeral. She had moved quickly all of her life. Her death came swiftly and surely. We felt that she hurried into heaven. But she slowed down the abbess' departure for an area that suffered a very severe ice storm the very day we would have been trying to achieve a site-decision there while traveling over icy roads in most unfavorable and even dangerous weather conditions. Remaining in Roswell an additional week to attend on the death and funeral of our determined Sister Aloysia, we then went on our mission to find that ice had yielded to sudden sunshine and eleven hours of site-searching made completely unhazardous. Without doubt Sister Aloysia was very pleased with how she had arranged things.

The first possible site we toured swept up to a hilltop amid small forest wilds. Sister Therese and I looked at each other several dozen times as we hiked through the small property whose rises and swoops of land made it appear large and sprawling. We knew what our hearts were saying. This is it. I seemed to expect our Father and Founder, St. Francis, to appear at any moment from behind one of the entanglements of trees reaching up to the heavens in an embrace of intertwined branches. We ran down steep inclines and puffed our way back up. And we knew.

We spent the rest of the day looking at the other sites under consideration. But eleven hours of inspection ended in a confirmation of our immediate early morning conviction. I telephoned back to Roswell. "We have an address", I said. All the Roswell sisters were gathered around our telephone's amplifier, again emphasizing our desire that, in this fashion at least, God readily endorsed: "We always want to be together."

A second set of foundresses was appointed after much prayer and announced with many tears. And on June 30, 1977, we set out for our new land. We have found that our understanding that the Blessed Sacrament, the Source of our strength, is indeed "the Food for our journey" concerns foundations, too. How does one survive another round of physical partings with the wounds of the first still so fresh upon the hearts of all? Only, we knew, in the presence of the Blessed Sacrament.

We bring the pain as also the joy of our human hearts into what we may oddly enough but profoundly and truthfully enough call the human Presence ("Body and Blood") of the Divinity ("Soul and Divinity"). We were acutely and salvifically aware of the human heart of Christ as we lined up on either side of the choir and passed our young foundresses from the embrace of one sister to the embrace of the next sister, while the organist played, over and over, the verses of the Church's special word of the Holy Thursday liturgy: "Ubi caritas et amor, Deus ibi est." Yes, he was there, the divine Master who was calling us forth and abroad again, right there at the center, our center.

I found myself wondering whether the human eyes of Christ had not misted over as he left his loved and immaculate Mother to begin his public life in which she was to appear only on the fringes and even this infrequently. Jesus was not playing at humanity, at humanism. Nor was Our Lady. I discovered myself wondering again whether there were not tears on her cheeks as she gave her Divine Son, whose humanity was born of her own, the *Pax* embrace of parting. The heart bears its own sworn testimony to truth. It is thus we know that Christ's immaculate Mother would not assume a less-than-human statuesque stand at this parting after thirty years of deepest human intimacy.

Often enough tears bear the truest testimony to love. We must have rendered good testimony that evening of June 29, 1977, as we prepared to send another little band of sisters forth and abroad. We thought of Clare, our Mother and Foundress, and of her younger sister, Agnes, who was sent forth and abroad from Assisi to Monticelli near Florence to be abbess of the community there. The one extant letter of Agnes to Clare is unequivocally clear about how Agnes felt at the human parting, the physical separation:

> It is a very great tribulation and immense sorrow for me physically and spiritually, and I am immeasurably weighed down and afflicted and almost unable to speak because I am bodily separated from you and the rest of my sisters with whom I believed I would live in this life and die. My tribulation indeed has its beginning but knows no end; it never knows when to stop but is always increasing; it began recently but reaches no end; it is always with me and never wants to depart.

The two sisters evidently mirrored true human-ism to each other. My thoughts returned in 1977 to St. Clare and St. Agnes of the thirteenth century as genuine mirrors of authentic humanism in their own lifetimes.

Into that space and down that path which opened out of the high Middle Ages into the burgeon-ing Renaissance had come two figures unlikely by worldly standards to become notable influences in the humanism just then beginning to gather its savants and its disciples into a new philosophy centered upon man. The young Assisian minstrel turned troubadour of God and the girl of aris-tocratic earthly plenteousness turned princess of poverty were to shine out first in Assisi and later throughout the world as entirely God-centered. Francis and Clare, the saints of Assisi, which be-came and remains world-famous simply because of their having lived there, might seem hardly to qual-ify as humanists. Yet, that is precisely what they were, in the most profound sense.

The newly reawakened fascination with the an-cient Greeks' accent on beauty, truth, and good-ness burst like a meteor upon the society of St. Francis' and St. Clare's time. It blossomed into a whole fresh galaxy of works of art, of music, of poetry. Men grew heady with the wine of their own achievements. And with continuing acceleration, men and women placed themselves at the center of creation. Thus falsely positioned, the glittering and intoxicating productions of mind and spirit that proliferated in the school of humanism cast their own shadow upon the very beauty they created, drew a web of unclarity over truth, and laid a threat to the goodness that can flourish only in God. All that was best in humanism as philosophy and attitude and life principle became endangered, often enough fatally so, by wrong positioning. The greatness of man sometimes tried to supplant the greatness of God. And the immediate result was the dwindling and drooping of mortal greatness after its re-rooting in un-Deific soil.

To St. Francis and St. Clare it was given as a readily historically recognizable reality to be outstanding Christian humanists. Whether as poet, his own eyes blind, singing a canticle to Brother Sun, whether as musician with his own kind of Stradivarius, whether as dramatist on Christmas Eve at Greccio, Francis sang, played, dramatized the centrality of God. Then, after him, came St. Clare. And today come after Clare the eighteen thousand strong who are called to be Clarian humanists, among them the tear-stained young humanists in the Roswell choir assembly of 1977. In the warmly affectionate gathering before the tabernacle that June evening, there was testified anew the humanism of the contemplative life centered on God, cloistered in God while yet reaching out to gather the whole world into an easy embrace, arms of concern stretched universal by reason of their "clinging to the poor Christ" (Second Letter of St. Clare to St. Agnes of Prague) as the center of their lives and the only meaning of all men's lives. Clinging to Christ, one necessarily embraces all mankind, since meaning and destiny lie in him alone.

Clare's God-centered humanism unfolds in every chapter of her brief Rule. Without ever abdicating her own authority, she consults her sisters in all matters of consequence, whether it be concerning the reception of new members, debts to be incurred, officials to be elected, or whatever. She presents unequivocal reminders to the sisters that from a vow of obedience there follows a strict obligation to obey. You made a promise to the Lord, declares Clare. Observe its consequences. Then, from this clearly articulated God-centered truth, she passes with ease to an equally lofty directive, humanistic in the deepest and most real sense: the abbess is to have "a close friendship" (Holy Rule, chapter 10) with all the sisters whom she is called and elected to serve as handmaid.

It is only in their God-centering that humanistic values can avail for growth and for happiness and be of any real human avail. Clare highly accents humanity, sometimes describing clearly its more inglorious expressions, as when she deals with serious offenders against the form of religious Profession who remain adamant in the face of the abbess' admonitions (Holy Rule, chapter 10), only to add almost airily that one ought not to worry about such things, as that would hinder love (ibid.). This woman of great heart and vistaed mind had a marvelously clear view of humanity's exalted possibilities and likely lapses, and this because she was centered in Christ. One assuredly gets a better perspective on the human condition when one has put on the mind of Christ, which is exactly what Clare did. Neither carried away by the exaltation of humanity nor disillusioned by the inadequacy of humanism as such, she became a clear mirror of true humanism, its possibilities made visible in Christ-centering, where its inadequacies are supplied by his saving grace and its failures redeemed in his Blood.

Thus, showing herself a clear mirror of true humanism, St. Clare was undeniably a high lyricist and a firm realist. She less speaks than sings as she invites her sisters to that glorious climax of humanism which is to be lifted above one's own human possibilities, as is decidedly necessary when a united community is invited by God to a physical parting with some of its members that he may have yet another tenting place upon the earth. "This is that height of most high poverty," she writes, "who has appointed you, my most dear sisters, heiresses and queens of the kingdom of heaven. . . . Let her who leads you into the land of the living be your portion. Totally clinging to her, most beloved sisters, desire for the name of Our Lord Jesus Christ and his most holy Mother to have nothing else forever under heaven" (Holy Rule, chapter 8).

The physical parting of membership in community can indeed be a testimony to that poverty in giving over to the call of God part of the on-site sisterhood. For Clare it was, as with St. Francis, always a matter of all or nothing. There existed for them no middle road of compromise. Half-heartedness was not for them whose human hearts are revealed to us as most truly human because of being identified with Christ. He calls. And we answer him. We go.

One has to exercise care, Clare cautions, if one is to exceed one's own possibilities by the power of Christ. What he gave, she declares, must gather interest. What it all reduces to and ascends toward, she sets down in a simple, all-demanding poetic reach beyond what secular humanism ambitions: "Always be lovers of God and of your souls and of all your sisters'' (Blessing of St. Clare). Perhaps it is just when the God we love calls physically forth and abroad from our midst the sisters whom we love that we can rejoice that we do love God with all our souls since clearly we would not otherwise part with sisters. Making a new foundation will necessarily call for exceeding one's own possibilities, given a loving and united community. "Well," we informed God again in June 1977, "we are indeed lovers of you, since we part only for you and at your summons"; ". . . and of all your sisters": "Well, God, we are making that clear enough."

We arrived at our destination on a very southernly July day. Many happy folk had assembled to welcome us and were clearly concerned that foundresses come from desert-dry New Mexico to their humid-high land might be more than a little disconcerted and begin musing on—the past. "This is about the hottest day in our history", one after another assured us with nervous emphasis. We were ready to believe it.

Enplaning and re-planing from Roswell, we had smiled to hear the sotto-whisper of plane attendants: "There are eight of them, and one has all the tickets." Each one of the founding six, however, had her own pledged heart's one-way ticket to our new foundation, and if there had been any doubt about a no-return, it would have been resolved when above the welcoming voices of milling folk and brighter than the camera flashes of newsmen, a priest's voice proclaimed: "Here he comes!" The crowds parted to let another priest come through. An immediate hush fell. For "he" was our Eucharistic Jesus humbly housed in a standing pyx under the humeral veil that covered his lodging on the heart of the priest from the parish church across the street. The Lord was conducted into his tabernacle-tent and enthroned there. We all fell upon our knees, pressed our foreheads to the floor and prayed that loved faith-affirmation dating from the thirteenth century and the beginning of our Franciscan Order, when Francis of Assisi first made it the manner and mode for himself and his followers upon coming into the presence of the Blessed Sacrament: "We adore you, O Lord Jesus Christ, here and in all your churches which are in the whole world."

All our souls were lifted up even as our bodies were prostrate in adoration. My poetic heart was lifted up to a high flight also. A year later I was to reveal said flight to the foundresses when I returned to them on visitation. "Oh! That moment! Oh! The thought that Jesus had one more Eucharistic tenting place on this earth! Oh! The wonder of a new foundation for his glory!" And, as I recall, I reviewed for them a few more of my

Oh's, adding: "I know you were all thinking the same thing." "*I* was thinking," replied one honest, unblinking foundress of one year, " 'Let's go home.' " After all, the Lord had a tenting place in Roswell, didn't he? But, in the end, no foundress ever turned back.

It was not in a monastery that we began Poor Clare life in our new land but in a very small convent generously lent to us by the parish, its former occupants, the teaching sisters, having just lately evacuated for want of personnel. But only a few blocks away was the enchanted forest where our monastery was one day to rise. We were permitted to go there on occasion for special reasons. One was for our first community chapter. Our long-suffering pastor loaded us and our accessories into his van and drove us to our new though yet invisible monastery some blocks away. Said accessories included a crucifix, two candles, a bench to serve as improvised altar, and our lunch. Which is not to say that we have lunch during chapter but only that we intended after that event to dine in our new invisible monastery.

A log was dragged into place under a tree for my convenience in delivering our first chapter conference ever. Seven stumps were gathered to serve as benches for the brethren. The sisters had thoughtfully set my log under a shade tree, and it was only

afterward that they informed me how a large scar-
let cardinal had sat quietly on a branch of that tree,
bent over me during the conference and hearing
me out to the end without so much as one wing-
flutter. It was, we agreed, a really nice touch of the
Lord.

Afterward there was time for private prayer and
for running up and down the slopes and finally
down the steepest incline to a plateau obviously
intended from the beginning of creation to be
our outdoors refectory. Then it was time to return to our mini-monastery. Our patient pastor
came to gather up ourselves and our belongings,
which had now notably increased by the addition
of some petrified woody stout vines that sent one
of our number, our ace carpenter-artist, into a semi-
rhapsodic state over the lectern she could (and indeed later did) make with the wood. Then, we had
discovered a few ancient apple trees still in labor
to bring forth some scant handfuls of wizened apples. But they were *our* apples from *our* trees on
our future monastery grounds. And we were very
proud of them. We had also dragged out of a semi-
impenetrable tangle of fallen branches, tree stumps,
and varied undergrowths some oddments of wood
we were sure could be coaxed and dreamed into
becoming benches for the little backyard of our
temporary dwelling that we proudly called "the

monastery garden". With these and other sundry trophies, we rode back in triumph with our heroic pastor, encouraging him to console himself with memories of how simple his life had been before he met the Poor Clares.

And so our cloistered life began again in a new setting. The ancient chants of the Divine Office rose out of the tiny makeshift choir six times each day and again at midnight. The Eucharistic Lord reigned in such grandeur as could be offered by the small standing pyx at daily exposition of the Blessed Sacrament. And there was a very solemn Mass to inaugurate all this and more.

The bishop and five priests, all splendid in gold vestments borrowed from the parish church, themselves filled the "public chapel" area while we occupied to capacity the cloister area. Our little organ, whose tender name, "Celestina", was proudly proclaimed on a small brass plate on her organic chest, found the long Mass too much for her. She gave a few final piteous gasps after the Gospel proclamation and then lapsed into a spent silence. The long prelude had quite exhausted her lung power. Those were happy days, though often rainbowed with tears. And then our permanent monastery began to rise.

Having returned to Roswell after the first weeks of foundation, come back for the groundbreaking in autumn of that same year, I flew back to our pioneers in November of 1978 to see the new monastery rising but not risen. The foundresses wanted to move in while I was there with them. This felicitous plan was thwarted by reason of the new monastery's not yet boasting a full roof and a few other such essentials. I could not remain until the lid was on and other small matters such as heating and plumbing installed and set functioning. We agreed to a symbolic moving-in. We would go to the unfinished monastery and have there all together, the whole eight of us, our first meal in the new monastery. And we would, all together, pray our first hour of the Divine Office there. And, all together, each would have a cell assigned to her in the dormitory.

So, we had a splendid soup cooked over a popcorn popper (feeling fulfilled to have found a use for the popcorn popper in an assembly where popcorn is not popped), said soup served on an impressive dining table of two boards set on two sawhorses conveniently left for our purpose, though unknown to them, by the workmen who had that day abandoned construction in deference to the cold. We prayed our Office before an altar hastily constructed from another loose-lying board. Dormitory cells were assigned to each one as planned. Despite their being at that point lacking in doors or windows, the cells, we agreed, were just perfect. What better boudoir could a Poor Clare have? We could not imagine. Later on, though, we were to discover that the county commissioners were not of the same persuasion. They could not, as upright county commissioners, agree to calling these Poor Clare dormitory dwellings "rooms". Our cells were listed as "sixteen closets".

Thus did monastic life go forward in our response to God's second "Forth and abroad!" Once while I and my traveling companion were on visitation of our young daughterhouse, thus again swelling the on-site personnel to eight, we had five pears. While such mathematical genius as is required for dividing five pears into eight portions is normally not mine, my joy in our littleness evidently raised me to an attainment ordinarily beyond me. With joyous exactitude I produced the eight portions, pondering how good it was to have what we might in our earlier lives have considered less than enough. Later on, though, when I attempted to share this joy with a visiting priest, his generous heart had a different perspective on poverty when it concerned his loved Poor Clares. Word went round. Benefactors have taken care that we do not need to exercise such mathematical feats again. The intriguing principle of "enough", however, we trust may ever undergird our lives.

"More!" is the word of an affluent society. More money, more ease, more pleasure, more leisure time, more space. It is altogether a pity to affix so beautiful a word as "more" to the very things that "more" renders destructive as a kind of dismal, dark, and sometimes deadly comment. For "more" in its essence belongs to God and the things that lead to God. It pertains to all that is true and good and beautiful, of which there can never be enough. More prayer is to be our happy response to our Lord's happily sweeping generality: "Pray always" (Lk 18:1). More love each year and each day is the blueprint for a happy marriage with more children to be its joy and its crown. More self-sacrifice is the responding word for every call to fill up in oneself "what is wanting in the sufferings of Christ" (Col 1:24). It is only when "more" is prefixed to what is basically destructive that it becomes a horror. From such misplacements issue more greed, more sensuality and self-debasement, more violence and crime to "fill in time", more frenetic haste to arrive at nothing.

It is the business of any and every Christian to situate "more" in its rightful place, to affix it to the "things that do not pass away". It is a particular business of enclosed nuns, every aspect of whose lives is designed to express in its own way that: God is enough!—and more than enough. The "more" of this is the radiant paradox of the cloistered contemplative life. There is an enclosure wall or some such setting off of a small compound destined to enclose the whole world in prayerful concern and sacrificial love. It is Christ's own love that marks the true "enclosure wall". "My beloved is a garden enclosed", we read in the Song of Songs (4:12). Yes, enclosed in his own suffering love for all mankind. He *is* the enclosure. That is why it is the most spacious place in the world.

Vast rolling acres are not needed for a setting apart in love. Just a little parcel of land is more than enough for occupants whose arms reach out to the whole world in prayer. And any one of the "sixteen closets" is vast enough for laying one's life down in love of God and his whole vast creation. After all, a Poor Clare's cell is just as large as the heart of its occupant, to whom it is assigned to reach out the alms of her dedicated life to the entire world. It is not so much that our small physical enclosure tells us where to stay as that it tells us where to go—out on spiritual mission to every needy and suffering heart in all the world. It needs only a small space to accommodate the greatest of all works, which is the complete surrender of the creature to God that he may use her just as he wills for his own large purposes.

We do not need much space when we have God.

Without him, the whole universe is crowded and cramped and even a stifling, graceless chamber. When the spirit is at home in God, we do not require things or space in which to roam, for the greatest expanse on all this earth and in the heavens, too, is the Heart of God. Enclosure in a little space as men may measure things is really just the radiant circle of the spirit at home in that small space made infinite by God.

And so it is, right down to the innocent enjoyment of the little good things of earth. Five pears can provide an orchardful of appreciation. A single cookie discovered under one's little dish in the refectory on a feastday is an event far beyond what any surfeit of sweets could offer. One same garment to wear on Sunday through Saturday makes for a wondrous wardrobe. And unshod feet are really more equipped for running both to God and to the spiritual needs of the whole world than well-shod ones. Simple living makes for large delights. Appreciation flowers well in the smallest garden plot.

Happy in these tested and proven convictions, we came in 1979 to the consummation of all things to be hoped for as concerns living quarters when our newly built monastery threw out its chest and announced that it was finished. We are allowed an "open house" after the Dedication Mass of a new monastery and before the papal enclosure is newly imposed. So, our dear neighbors from close by and other sundry parts came "in" after the Mass to inspect with loving interested eyes our physical compound. Only some eyes got misted over. "Oh, so small, those cells!" kind benefactors bewailed them. But, no! Why, each one was of such expanse as to contain a homemade straw mattress set on its three boards, a little washstand/workstand, a cheerful small bench, and—a window! Yes, a window letting in the variant whole of the changing skies. Later there would even be little wooden cupboards for Poor Clare living essentials. In the beginning we constructed cupboards out of cardboard boxes. For the most part these fulfilled well their noble task, with some rather notable exceptions, as when in the middle of the night one of them collapsed under the weight of the earthly goods of that cell's occupant and lay in its disastrous ruin on the head of the erstwhile dreaming foundress. While holding firmly to our conviction that "a little is enough" and to our affection for makeshifts, we did lose our confidence in cardboard as being an outstanding construction material.

When came the time to confess that we truly needed to have a larger chapel and choir, there appeared again that loved prelate from Rome, Archbishop Augustine Mayer, O.S.B., on business in the United States and drafted into the business of first groundbreaking for the new prayer quarters. Shovel in hand, the Archbishop made the first excavation for the choir. It was a cold, windy March day. But our hearts were warm with grateful joy and zephyred breezes of appreciation that we should have such honor done us.

Archbishop Mayer had been well given to appreciate the need for a larger choir by previous experience in the temporary choir. We had thought to spare him the struggle to survive a canonical hour of the Divine Office while wedged into a choir stall of notably smaller proportions than is usual for Curial officials at St. Peter's in Rome or for abbots at a vast Metten Abbey in Germany. To actuate the desired convenience, we had inducted into our very small choir a prie-dieu and a chair for His Excellency. *Voila!* The remaining difficulty regarded a method for propelling myself to the organ and back again as rubrics would indicate without disturbing Archbishop Mayer.

I thought to save His Excellency inconvenience by favoring my own, at no time a feat easy of attainment, since it has been made clear to us as to others privileged to know him that if in any situation there is going to be inconvenience, it is going to be for him and not for anyone else. Still, I assayed a brave attempt. This, however, was only to discover that my fleetest movement toward the organ, with all possible flattening of my person against the wall so as not to disturb His Excellency, was doomed to swift failure as the alert Archbishop sprang to his feet and stepped aside and out of our one and only guest prie-dieu so that I might easily pass. Yes, we did need a larger choir. And it was a wondrous thing to have Archbishop Augustine Mayer preside at a devotional groundbreaking for it.

And wondrous is sisterhood in Poor Clare living, anchored in God. Anchor is a word we like. One is fastened to where one is and has chosen to be. Our second foundation was now established, the permanent monastery built. And, not in words but in a low humming in our hearts, was the assurance that God had now said: "Enough!" as regards new foundations and fresh partings. We breathed easily as we set out to recover from previous pains of sending forth sisters. We were not, however, to be given time for long, deep breaths. Only deep, not long.

Chapter III

Out West

St. Francis and St. Clare may not belong in the same category of discoverers as Christopher Columbus, but discoverers they were, daily engaged in discovering and rediscovering the love of God and his goodness and his ever-creative beauty, the potential of man, the beauty of the universe, and other such things sundry. Sighting a sprawling new continent or being stopped by a small bird heralding spring were, in the most profound sense, all the same to them. Both reduced to a matter of a great Creator-God and his small folk daily discovering his creation.

It might be thought there is not much to discover in a cloister. A meager assortment of acres set within walls could hardly have much to offer toward setting the pulses racing with the thrill of new discoveries or for begetting a holiday spirit.

The fact is, however, that the two holidays in the year available to us for world travel via the library, scholarly research in that same quarter, and great Poor Clare advances in musicology, astronomy, literary composition and the like are events so glorious as to be called "discovery days". And the fact that the world travel, the research, and the great outreaches of the arts and sciences all take place within the cloister is at the heart of the meaning of discovery.

Discovery days were initiated quite some years back when it was revealed to cloistered nuns by a whole new contingent of psychologists that they (that is, the cloistered nuns, be clear) were inhibited in their unbearably circumscribed lives and must begin to take holidays. Wishing to maintain recognition as being avant-garde folk, we instituted holidays. Only we didn't go anywhere. Why should we? There is more material within enclosure walls for the discovery that is at the heart of all genuine holidays than can be measured.

So, we decided on two holidays a year. This meant that, aside from the eight-plus hours spent in liturgical and private prayer, the time needed for the domestic chores of the day, meals, and two portions of sleep—a few hours before the midnight Office and a few hours after—the day was all free for holiday, discovery, new frontiers.

St. Francis could rhapsodize over a bird in flight, and St. Clare over a leafing tree. Both their seraphic hearts traveled by prayer and love the whole world, so dearly small to their Godlike spirits. Enraptured by the beauty of creation thrown like a thin veil over the Face of God, Francis wrote his great poem, "The Canticle of the Creatures". Dying Clare called out to God: "I thank you, Lord, for having created me." And then called out to her soul: "Go ahead securely, my soul, for you will have a good companion on your journey." Yes, God was an ever-present good companion to St. Francis and St. Clare. And each of them to him. Their lives were a continual holiday of love, lives sometimes suffering, sometimes rejoicing, always singing. It took so little to make them happy. And the little made them large with love.

So, what do daughters of these two great discoverers do on holiday, on a "discovery day"? At the last one in Roswell, our beloved octogenarian went off to Chartres in France via the written story of its cathedraled wonders and gave all the rest of us at recreation that evening a marvelous mini-lecture on beauty in color and form and glorious enterprise. A silver jubilarian invaded outer space by a day-long study of what is busying God outside the small confines of earth. Some advanced the cause of spiritualizing Western horticulture by devoting

lengths of time and profundity of consideration
to earnest little verbenae pushing up through the
gravel paths and plump hyacinths prevailing over
winter. One determined scholar got a high stool,
established herself upon it before the stand that
holds Noah Webster's modest word study, and read
the dictionary all day. Words are, after all, intoxicating for the mind and the spirit, being struck
off the Word of God. The holiday spirit stirred everywhere, even to the encouraging of one intrepid
soul, inspired to begin learning the violin, to go to
the farthest end of the garden to initiate her career
on the strings. A beginning violinist must have privacy, we agreed, for the sake of her sisters.

It is part of the reward of having little as men
might appraise things that Poor Clares become
facile discoverers of much that could perhaps go
unnoticed by those who have many things and
much time and little joy. There must be a singing
poverty, conglomerate with whatever walk of life,
if one is to discover the wonders of life too often
left unnoticed in the pursuit of the non-wondrous
ephemeral, the non-satisfying surfeit. There is evidence enough that having too much, we enjoy too
little. It needed one as poor in things as Francis of
Assisi to appreciate all things. Continually amazed
at the wonder of creation, he was ready to grow
lyrical over a little stream of water in the woods

that provided him beverage and the broken pieces of bread he had begged that spread out for him a banquet. His companion at that particular picnic, Brother Masseo, lagged rather noticeably behind Francis in being a discoverer. It was not Masseo's idea of a really good picnic. He was to have his ideas enlarged and perspectives broadened, however, by living with St. Francis. Discoverers beget discoverers. And there is a desperate need for their tribe to increase. For God's creation, whether cosmic or Lilliputian, cries out to be discovered by his sentient creatures. What is required of an ardent discoverer is to have nothing of excess, little of baggage, and an arc lamp of eager love in the heart.

So, what do we do on "discovery day"? We discover and rediscover the wonders of God and of one another and of the physically small and spiritually sprawling environs of our cloistered lives. There are two things notable about holidays: (1) The fewer they are per se, the more do they establish themselves in the everyday, preparing us through the ever-opening new wonders of things for the eternal wonder of paradise. (2) They are best situated in one's own dwelling, the wonders of which can so easily be overlooked by reason of frequent excursions out of it.

One of our greatest discoverers was our late Sister Annuntiata, presently and eternally engaged in discovering heaven. Only she was never late and could not be so now. A young postulant, writing to her parents, set herself to describe our community to them. There was Mother Abbess, thus and so. Mother Vicaress, thus and so. The mistress of novices, thus and so. Her young companions in the novitiate, thus and so. "And," she wrote, "there is a little very old sister; and she is the queen of the whole place." Indeed. Sister Annuntiata went home to God one February. And, as she did everything else, she did it swiftly. Her last hours we hold for a flower on our hearts as we listen for the little cane no longer tapping along to the choir and the hum of the sewing machine so strangely silent now.

Sister Annuntiata had entered the cloister at the age of eighteen. She knew her own mind early. And she knew her own mind all her life. For it was always God's mind to which she hearkened and responded. During her religious life she held many offices and performed many services. She was cook, infirmarian, portress, mistress of novices. And then, at the age of fifty-nine, she hearkened to a new expression of the mind of God, which was that he wanted a new tabernacle in Roswell, New Mexico. With her companion since novitiate days, Mother Immaculata, who was to be abbess in the new foundation in Roswell for many years, Sister Annuntiata set out to discover unknown New Mexico.

An old farmhouse was purchased and revamped into a monastic edifice. A big vegetable field was planted. Flowerbeds were laid. Nuns' cells were arranged. A tiny refectory was wedged in. It all went quickly. Things always went quickly when Sister Annuntiata was "on project". A rancher's cows were our only close neighbors those first years. And Sister Annuntiata was solicitous about those cows. When we young ones had gathered bushel basketfuls of luscious green weeds, we were instructed to take them to the back wire fence then supplying for the enclosure wall we could not yet afford to complete and to feed them to the appreciative cows. It was always like that, her solicitude for every living creature. And that was a fortunate Poor Clare, a blessed priest, a favored person, a lucky pussycat or cow who crossed her path and was discovered by her all-loving gaze.

She was indeed a legend in her own lifetime. Remaining in the demanding office of mistress of novices until she was seventy-five years of age, she also remained ever just a bit too swift for young postulants or novices to keep up with her. When she retired from that office, she was elevated by our love and esteem to her lifelong office of example for and mentor to us all. She became truly "the queen of the whole place", as the new postulant had quickly discovered her to be. I recall another young postulant who had been darkly warned by certain persons before she entered the cloister that an exuberant personality like hers would be quickly "flattened out" in such a life. It was not for her. She was too alive. I asked Virginia after the first several weeks how she was getting along. She remarked with cryptic and affectionate accuracy: "Well, I've been observing Sister Annuntiata. She's been in the cloister for sixty years now, and she's certainly not flattened out."

As she entered into her late eighties and gradually surrendered certain of her work activities, so that we no longer heard the washing machine giving off its chug-chug before the rest of us had rubbed the sleep from our eyes at 5:00 A.M. or observed her making her famous "health cookies" when we had all been working hard in the garden all morning, she began sewing "in earnest". That is to say, the sewing machine began turning out hundreds and hundreds of the bright little aprons that became the best-seller in our small gift shop. To her little workroom, which was built like a round tower and overlooked the garden on three sides so that she could keep a close eye on all growing things, whether postulants, spinach, or the honey locust trees she so especially loved, we all came as to a magnet of splendid Poor Clare-edness. She had special privileges because of her great age and great wisdom and great holiness. And so the sisters could go and speak to her about their charges, their plans, their interests, their aspirations. It was a mecca for the young, that little tower workroom. In our community of mostly very young religious, she knew no generation gap. Nor did they. It was not so much that she was age-mellowed with wisdom. Nor that she was so young in heart. It was more that she was ageless. She belonged to every generation because she was so totally God's.

She became quite deaf with the years. But it would never do that she should not hear every word at chapter or recreation or whatever. We discovered that she could be "channelled in" by way of a tape recorder. And so, at chapter or at classes or conferences, her little red earphones set in place, she would sit at earnest attention, quick to let any speaker know that she or he was not coming through and should "speak more clearly". Bishops, priests, abbesses have been thus admonished. She just never wanted to miss out on anything in community. Again, because she was so totally God's, she was totally a community person. And first of all in the large community of the Church. None of the liturgical changes of recent

years troubled her. How often we heard her familiar "Let's go!", whether it was time to help her
down to choir for Office or to recreation or for a
ride out in the garden in her little blue chair. "Let's
go!" And for whatever new idea Holy Church set
before us, it was for her nothing but "Let's go!"
She knew how to keep the old and welcome the
new. She read modern theologians and devotional
writers of past centuries and quoted from both at
our recreations with equal ease and appreciation.
When the whole breviary was redone and the rest
of us took up one part after another until we had
familiarity with its entire schema, she was, as always, 'way ahead of us. She simply mastered it all
in one lesson or two, so eager was she. God had
gifted her with keen intelligence, and she honed
it all her life. God had created her heart so loving
and giving, and she exercised it all her life.

We have reading during our meals. A young religious would begin. But then Sister Annuntiata
would ascend the reader's dais to continue. Every
dinner. Each collation. She read with volume, emphasis, and occasional marginals of her own. Then
she would be off to choir for her adoration hour,
never to be missed, for so many extra visits to
the Blessed Sacrament, with the familiar tap-tap of
the cane announcing her passage toward the Eucharistic Jesus who was so obviously the Center

of her life. When there were occasional visits of
the entire community to the parlor on a special
occasion, she had good counsel for all. The Archbishop was told to stand firmly with the Pope. The
Franciscan Provincial was given to understand the
importance of discipline in the seminaries. Priests
were admonished to pray to their guardian angels.
When we built our newest wing, she studied every
blueprint and advised the architect and contractor
from her great fund of marvelous good sense and
in her inimitable way. Everyone listened. Everyone loved her. Everyone prized her.

Life was so intensely interesting to Sister Annuntiata. It held unlimited possibilities for her loving
heart as she saved up honey locust seeds to send to
missionaries in India so that there would be beauty
and shade for the poor, or informed me that for
twenty-five dollars she could buy a goat for a poor
leper in Africa, or laid out her own garden plans
for our newest foundation.

Sister Annuntiata's great heart for the Church
and the world went on ever expanding. She had
mastered the scriptural directive to "pray always
and without ceasing". There were always two
sounds to hear as any of us entered her workroom: the hum of the sewing machine and the
soft murmur of her prayer. It was always either:
"Jesus!" or "Hail, Mary". And so she lived until

that last week, that last day of her earthly life. A
young nun's brother was to be married, and she
finished an apron for his bride-to-be. The father
of our young infirmarian who looked after Sister
Annuntiata in her little personal needs had just had
surgery, and Sister Annuntiata was earnestly blessing him with holy water, flung out in his direction with her generous hand each night before she
retired. The Holy Father was in Nigeria, and her
thoughts, her prayer were right there with him.
Our hospital was having the government inspec-
tors in for the regular visit, and her grateful prayers
were overseeing the inspection. She told a young
novice for a final time to turn up her habit sleeves
a second time when washing off the tables. She
reminded Mother Abbess, who had once been her
postulant and novice, to be sure to take long, deep
breaths for strength and relaxation. She was "for
others" unto the end.

Then, one day after dinner, she said that she did
not feel well. We thought she had better rest for
a while. So, she flung the familiar blue apron over
the back of her chair and went off to obey, to rest.
But that evening she still did not feel well. Our
frequent little loving consultations with her would
invariably bring a typical response: "I am so well
cared for . . . I was just praying for those poor old
women dying on the streets of India with no one to

care for them or love them. Thank God for Mother Teresa!'' Yes, ''for others'', unto the end.

The next morning she was up, preparing for Holy Mass, but feeling so weak that we persuaded her not to come down. Obediently, she lay down again. Then our wonderful doctor decided he had better take some X rays. We sent our precious sister off around noon. The last word the little group of sisters hurriedly assembling around her heard (we did not convoke the whole community, for she was ''only going for some X rays'') was again precisely typical: ''Gasoline is so expensive these days, and now they have to drive out here to get me and take me to the hospital!'' And, naming the administrator and superior there, she added: ''What would we ever do without them!''

Because of Sister Annuntiata's advanced age and weakened condition and also mindful of her advanced deafness, we sent our young infirmarian along with her. When doctor wished to keep her overnight in the hospital, we felt Sister Infirmarian should remain to assist our cherished eldest. All seemed well in the late evening. Sister Annuntiata was feeling better. Everything was ''satisfactory''. Yes, and more than we knew! For only two hours later, at 10:30 P.M., the call came from the hospital: a very sudden change. The abbess and vicaress whom Sister Annuntiata had guided in Poor Clare living since their postulant days went quickly to the hospital, arriving at 11:15. "She is dying", the hospital superior said, with classic simplicity and love. We prayed the litany for the dying and other prayers of Holy Church that are so fortifying. Our sister was breathing easily and quietly now, though very slowly. But the delicate little hands were parchment white and the fingernails blue. One could only repeatedly kiss those hands stretched out in love, folded in prayer, busy with labor for seventy-three years of Poor Clare living.

"And at midnight a shout was raised: 'Behold! the Bridegroom comes! Go out to meet him!' " And so that is exactly what Sister Annuntiata did, as I held her in my arms. Surely Jesus took up her own word: "Let's go!" And she enthusiastically responded: "Oh, yes!—let's go!" It was so gentle, that swift passing into eternity. No agony, no struggle, no pain in those last hours. She was always so quick in life. She was quick in death.

So, we came home, carrying the familiar cane with us. And we laid the cane on the altar step. She did not need it now. She lay in lovely state for two days. And we went from choir to her cell, where, beside her crucifix and little pictures on the wall, hung a map of the country. She had "prayer intentions" for every State of the Union. The map was so significant. Her heart was so large. And from her cell we went, irresistibly drawn, to her little tower workroom. There was one apron, put down in haste. The sewing machine open, an apron string under the foot of the needle. A mission magazine open beside her chair. We could hardly bear to enter the little room. We could not stay out of it. We did not begrudge her that swift flight to eternal joy, but we ached with missing her.

The Mass was a triumphal crown on her long life of utter fidelity to God and Holy Church, her community and all the world. Our Archbishop was the principal concelebrant. During the homily, he looked through the wide-spaced altar grille at her sleeping figure and said: "Blessed are you among women, Sister Annuntiata!" All of our Franciscan friars came to express in the glorious Mass that love they had had for her in life. And the diocesan priests came, too. And her family. And our doctors, our lawyer, our contractor, our workmen, our hospital leaders, and so many friends. "May the angels lead you into paradise!" we sang, remembering her profound devotion to the angels, who could surely never have more joyously led a procession into paradise. And, at the burial vault, the white-chasubled priests and ordained deacons stood like a circle of angels around her body, our loved episcopal shepherd, crozier in hand, eyes liquid with love and esteem, at her feet. The tower bells pealed and pealed for her entrance into eternity. The organ filled the sunlit morning with its great nuptial march.

We sang the final prayer to Our Lady of Guadalupe: "Make love burn brightly in our hearts all days, until you bring us safely to the vision of your Most Holy Son." She was lifted into the vault. And then the friars sang their traditional "Ultima in hora mortis nostræ", and we sang with them, their strong and beautiful voices resounding against the burial vault, spreading over the sunlit morning. We had each asperged her with holy water, the sacramental she so loved and valued. She was joyously drenched with it. A honey bee circled over her. A single lark looked down from the overhanging tree.

Then we went slowly back into the house, determined to try to carry on her glorious tradition of true Poor Clare living and use well this legacy left us by so great a sister.

One legacy she left us was the clear proclamation of another "Forth and abroad!" a few years before she departed to add her inimitable self to our celestial foundation. Supposing ourselves to be in a kind of emotional recovery period after our 1977 foundation, we began to shift about uneasily in mind and in heart over something that sounded very much like That Voice again, this time strongly suggesting that recovery would be best achieved at this point by some strenuous exercise of the heart and spirit. It was 1979.

Set atop a hill in the flowering West of our land was an uniquely charming monastery, branches of the main trunk of the edifice spreading out in many directions like arms reaching to gather new young members to its Eucharistic heart. There were fruit trees perseveringly bearing their beauteous oranges and lemons and grapefruits. There was a rose garden whose fragrance had assuredly wafted down from heaven. The old building twisted and turned in singular creativeness, its corridors sloping up and down in a kind of playfulness, inviting the community procession to lower its collective head and charge the uphill or to resort to its brakes on the downhill. In so much of the picturesque there was one thing wanting: members. Deaths and difficulties had reduced the brave little community to so small a number as to draw a dark question mark across its future. A courageous and wonderful abbess faced the fact and asked for help. Our hearts went out to her and her valiant little crew, reached out to the charming monastery seeming from its high hilltop perch to be awaiting recruitment from—where?

Even as we compassionated and prayed, we knew, of course, that personnel could not come from us. We met in community conference to consider what could possibly be done, from where help might be summoned, what proposals could be made. Although by this time well entered into the age of consensus and also well admonished by how many religious periodicals against decisions arrived at outside series upon series of debative discussions, we yet had one discussant tailored by Providence to exercise the overpowering strength of simple truth. At age ninety-one, Sister Annunti-ata had a fresh, clear outlook on life and all its situations. She was also gifted by God with remarkable clarity of expression. It would, of course, be completely predictable for our loved nonagenarian to declare that a monastery of mostly young sisters, ranks reduced by two foundations within one decade, obviously was not able to give personnel assistance elsewhere at such a time. However, Sister Annuntiata had never really been predictable except for piercing spiritual insights and energetic conclusions. So, we found ourselves newly pierced with enlightenment and our Poor Clare motors recharged.

Her approach to all things and sundry had always been direct and clear. It was very direct and quite clear as she turned her gaze slowly from one sister to another seated around our community room table. When we had all been thus thoroughly examined, she made her speech. It consisted of one sentence. "If a community God has blessed like this one", she began, "let a little suffering community go under, God ought to curse us." Her message thus made clear and concluded, she announced that it was time for her to go to the choir for adoration. And off she went. A few weeks later off we went, too, in the persons of two young nuns to be followed later by two more of our number. Out West to the monastery on the hilltop.

God, who had long since and severally shown us how in accord with Sister Annuntiata's thinking was his own, gave new proof of his divine approbation. We watched a courageous, faith-filled abbess on that hilltop grow young again. Two young applicants shortly presented themselves, entered, and remained. Eleven other new members have followed them. And Sister Annuntiata, we are confident, is eternally pleased that her intervention at a Roswell community meeting in 1979 was so availing.

She was always a great discoverer, whether it was to capture a locust and have him for lunch in order to know just what St. John the Baptist's menu had to offer for New Mexico desert dwellers in the twentieth century, or to devise new and improved methods of gardening for the community's hope-for-the-future who entered into novitiate life without lore of the land. She evidently discovered, upon arrival in eternity, that the founding group there needed increased membership. For gentle Sister Tarcisius went to join the quartet only one month after Sister Annuntiata had gone to get things moving beyond the skies.

When Sister Tarcisius had begun failing physically, the doctor informed us that it was imperative that she exercise. Walk. Move. Our shy beloved was not at all enthusiastic about this and viewed the changing love-guard of the young sisters who came in turn each day to "take her for a walk" with a marked lack of, if not *joie de vivre*, assuredly *joie de marcher*. But there was a magic word: obedience. "Mother Abbess wants you to walk." And after a few suspicious questionings as to whether Mother Abbess had actually said this and it could be proven true, off she would go on this new mileage of obedience.

Gently she lived, gently she died. But only when the actual hour arrived, not at the predictable earlier hours. Like the time she collapsed in the choir, was anointed right there by our devoted chaplain (who raced out to the monastery when we raised the alarm), and was thence carried to the chapter room until she could be taken to the infirmary. She lay there, eyes closed, breathing nearly imperceptible, with us watching beside her as we awaited the doctor's arrival. It was an intensely dramatic vigil around our loved sister, whose consciousness had obviously already left all things of earth. Or so we thought, until she suddenly opened her eyes, gazed at the loving vigilantes around her, and inquired briskly: "How are things going in the foundations?" Or like another time when we wondered if the Father Confessor were going to make it for her final anointing, as she lay on her bed, clearly more dead than alive. But Father did make it. And Sister Tarcisius opened her eyes, studied his visage, and began chatting amiably with him in German, a language she knew was as familiar to him as to herself. Sometimes unpredictable she was in her lovable ways. Wholly predictable was her unfailing gentleness. Surely she enhanced our heavenly foundation with her unique presence when she responded to God's final "Forth and abroad!" to her and went off to discover his eternal love.

It was a year since our going out West. The years henceforward would assuredly never discover us going anywhere else.

Chapter IV

A Beautiful City

Deepest down in every human being there lies a beautiful city. And as all true human striving labors toward uncovering it, so the most tragic of all human failures is to leave it undiscovered. All of the spiritual life pertains to archaeology, as layer upon layer within us is arduously removed to reveal what lies beneath and whose wonder must be seen to be believed. It is painstaking digging that brings to the spent and weary archaeologist of the soul a joy that needs no describing to those who have known it and that cannot be explained to those who have not.

Hopefully, we each of us arrive at a point of spiritual ennui with life in the city of the convenient half-measures so inconvenient for the experience of joy. If we allow it to ourselves, we shall eventually arrive at the experience of salvific weariness with our excuses for our mediocrity. It grows so tiresome always to be explaining away our pitiable subterfuges.

The falsity of pretense cobbles the streets of this city, too. There is the espoused false goal of maturity considered as a state of indifference to rejection or non-acceptance, to ingratitude or facile forgetfulness, to non-understanding and easy discord. There is the concept of impassivity as a spiritual triumph. The state of non-caring as a human victory. But there comes, if we allow it, the day when the stripped soul and aching heart find this city of spiritual make-believe intolerable. We begin, desperately enough, to uncobble these streets, to lift-and-lower and lower-and-lift the strong pick of reality until, weary but determined, we stand at last amid the rubble of falsity, heart quickening to the rising certainty that something worth the digging lies below all this.

And so the spiritual archaeologist, driven and unflagging, perseveres in the hard sweating of the soul until the outlines of an ancient city buried beneath finally appear. A city of truth where confrontation with reality begets, not despond, but a quickening of the heart, the soul, and the body as well. We set ourselves to search about in this buried and perhaps long-buried city of reality for the true meaning of ourselves. And it begins to take shape.

False goals are often easily enough achieved, and this because the facile dark victory of their achievement is far removed from the effort required to face and confess the power of our fellow human beings to wound and debilitate us. It was not so with Christ, who confides to us in the Gospel the hurt of his perfect human heart over ingratitude, rejection, and that whole company of wounds. "Did I not work this miracle for ten? Where are the nine? Only this stranger has come back to thank me" (Lk 17:17, 18). Or, "What have I done? My people, how have I offended?" (Good Friday Liturgy). And so much else. It is necessary to be an archaeologist in the layers of our protective self-defenses in order to allow our gaze to come upon the vulnerable Christ-image deep within the human heart he has shaped for each individual one of us.

Reality brings its own rewards, which are unknown to the self-evasion that lies in layer upon layer over the beautiful city at the most profound level of every human being. "Forth and abroad!" finds its most painful but likewise most rewarding reality in that arrival at the root of one's own being, in the "abroad" of that sighting of the inmost reality of one's own creation. Deep, deep down is the beautiful city of each human being. And when the overlays of pretense and falsity and evasion are dug away, there appears, out from under, that beautiful city of God's creation of a person made in his own image and likeness and thus a dazzlingly lovely vision to behold.

Part of cloistered contemplative living deals directly with spiritual archaeology. The very close living that the cloister provides offers a marvelous aid, if we will accept it, in digging through the ruins of our shared sinfulness and spiritual fragility toward the perhaps half-buried or at least well-covered-over truths about ourselves. Each human "city" in the cloister emerges quickly enough from the layers of self-delusion that could perhaps be long nurtured in a less intense company. Without any actual intent to do so, each nun by her very closeness to each other nun is digging down toward the basic reality of the other. That is why cloistered living must abound in love. We are all of us more than sensitive about having our "ruins" exposed to the light as just that: ruins. Nor can we long tolerate any personalized archaeology save that of true love. The ruins overlaying the original beautiful city that is God's idea of each of us resents and repulses a shovel not held in a loving hand.

Cloistered living is a training in basics. And the basic sisterhood of a community as a whole as well as the sisterly love of each individual are revealed perhaps nowhere more clearly than when some of the company of the on-site archaeologists are called to another enterprise or, to put it more accurately, to continue the same enterprise in other quarters. Thus, to our initial incredulity and continuing amazement, God sounded again in 1986 his now familiar but nonetheless hearts-devastating call to go forth. And it really was to a Beautiful City.

This time the call first sounded through layfolk who knew the Roswell community well and who also knew about foundations being made from there. It was proposed in 1985 to their bishop by these same layfolk that their beautiful city was wanting in one aspect: it had no cloistered nuns. We could agree that such a reality was altogether a shame and that someday somebody from some monastery should do something about it. Our community was obviously not within consideration. Our poor hearts were still committed to daily spiritual deep-breathing exercises to try to maintain emotional equilibrium after two and a half foundations (which is to say, two foundations and one rebuilding) in little more than a dozen years. We knew that our surface reasons against foundational egress at this time were sound. Our upper cognitive archaeological layer offered solid enough ground for the conclusions to whose cadences our hearts yearned to march. Only there came again that unsettling concern. Could it be? Was it possible? We knew we had to make some excavations. Under the upper and itself beautiful city of sisterhood bonded in one dwelling lay the supporting strata of sisterhood bonded in the Will of God. And it was spelling out another: "Forth and abroad!"

Often enough the large emotional weights on the heart can be counterbalanced not so much by consideration, argument, or debate as by the kindly dictation of pressing practical considerations. If God wished us situated in another new cloister, we could readily deduce that there had to be some semblance at least of a cloister situation. And that the monastery could not be suspended in air but must needs have some solid ground on which to stand.

The bishop described with a wistful sigh the beautiful stretch of land he had been viewing with a studied and eager eye. But for what he knew such land would cost, it might as well have been in outer space considering his and our finances or lack of same. It seemed to me the time to instruct our bishop-to-be in the ways of Franciscan Finance as established by our Father and Founder, St. Francis of Assisi.

In the thirteenth century, Francis needed to rebuild a little church in Assisi. In fact, God had made it quite clear to Francis that he was to rebuild the church, even going so far as to speak to young

Francis from the crucifix then hanging in the tottering little church of San Damiano. The fact that he had neither skill of stone masonry in his head nor ready cash in his hands was not the kind of difficulty to give Francis of Assisi pause. His own kind of businessman, he went about the streets of Assisi, proposing a splendid and obviously sound bargain: "He who gives me a stone will have a blessing from God. He who gives me two stones will receive two blessings." We can presume that this salesmanship mounted into the multiple blessings certain to descend upon those who gave multiple stones "for free". Francis got his stones and rebuilt his church. And the great crucifix from which the voice of the crucified Christ had directed: "Francis, go and rebuild my church, which, as you see, is falling into ruins" is enthroned to this day in the Basilica of Santa Chiara in Francis' native town of Assisi.

Enthroned in the souls of each of his vast progeny of sons and daughters is the awesome full revelation of that message to Francis from the crucifix of the little church that he did indeed rebuild. This pertained to the same spiritual rebuilding of the very Church of God in which thousands upon thousands of his spiritual sons and daughters through the past eight centuries have been and still are involved.

A Beautiful City of God lies deep in every human heart, ever needing, in some measure, a rebuilding. Right then, in early 1986, however, a pressing immediate concern was a material abode for the Eucharistic Christ and for those who would come to adore him and offer their lives for the help and healing of an injured world. Yes, it was clearly time to assist the bishop in procuring land for this abode.

The bishop attended patiently and politely on my instruction in the field of business administration and purchase. He agreed, half-bemused, to inquire whether the owners of the property that had caught his eye and his heart would like to make it a gift to the cloistered Poor Clare nuns coming to found a new monastery. And so this newest piece of Franciscan business enterprise proceeded. Maybe the owners really would give a reduction on the price of the land. Perhaps even a large reduction for such unusual business as cloistered nuns coming to set up a house of prayer for the world and day-and-night adoration of God. Only the owners would not give any reduction on the land. They gave the land to us. An outright gift to the Poor Clare nuns who needed a place to pray for all the world, beginning with the folk of their diocese. "They said that they would *give* it to you", the bishop repeated to me several times, like a man in a dream but not desirous of being awakened. After this, we could only conclude that we had heard aright: God wanted a Poor Clare monastery there, and we were the ones he had in mind. Like folk more than somewhat dazed, we went, two of us, to look at the situation.

The situation consisted of long rolling lawns with giant pines marking off the perimeters. It included a lake where ducks inspected us and apparently approved us, as they returned calmly in short order to their preferred hydro-olympics. The property featured so sharp a drop at the back as to exclude any need for an enclosure wall at that juncture of the land. No creature of larger proportions or lesser agility than a spider could ever ascend the sheer drop and invade the enclosure. This, we knew, was it: God's newest acre for us to set up Poor Clare housekeeping.

For the year and a half of the new monastery's rising, we lived in a convent vacated by sisters of the active apostolate. It had to become an enclosed mini-monastery, and the many dire predictions that "people will never understand this enclosure business" eventuated only in new evidence that layfolk will both understand and appreciate the papal enclosure of contemplative nuns in whatever measure the nuns themselves understand and appreciate it. There was no consideration of building an enclosure wall around a temporary property. But they had built us a tall fence. And when we arrived, *tout en force*, on June 4, 1986, we found that the dear folk of our new diocese had lined the wooden enclosure fence with hanging baskets of flowers. It was, we thought, a really "nice" touch.

We had arrived in high state, which is to say: in a rented mini-bus that had taken us into its capacious hospitable arms at the airport. The bishop's exuberant presbyteral secretary had filled it with balloons. These burst, each in turn, into demise along the highway as the lurching bus brought them into contact with the pins in nuns' veils, affording a dramatic sound track for *new foundation scenario*, as in a different mode of expression the hanging baskets set the lovely scene.

The property adjoining ours was a home for retired priests. Save when one came occasionally to replace our regular chaplain at Mass or Benediction, they never saw us. So it was indeed food not just "for thought" but for marveling prayer that when one of them gave us a substantial gift toward the building of our permanent monastery, he said only: "I have been observing you." He could only have observed a silent presence vibrant with love. For our falling in love with our new beautiful city and its beautiful citizens was a state that had come to be abiding, as into the rivulets of tears in our hearts at leaving Roswell there entered the tributary stream of joy at making another tenting place on earth for our Eucharistic Lord. Evidently the stream was visible, for our new pastor told us he had confided to his parishioners from the pulpit: "I have met the happiest people in the world. They live down the street at the new Poor Clare monastery."

Yet there were for the foundresses the inevitable hard weeks and months of returning raw nostalgia for the mother monastery in Roswell. To ease the rawness came the loved figure of now-Cardinal Augustine Mayer, O.S.B., true "father of his little ones". There was Holy Mass offered by His Eminence in the minuscule chapel at the elfin-sized altar with the same dignity and majesty as at a Mass in St. Peter's Basilica in Rome. Truly, we are who we are and what we are wherever we are. And this eminent Churchman, scholar, abbot, teacher is predominantly spiritual father. His admonition to the little founding group after breaking ground for the new permanent monastery is cherished to this day: "Step by step, grace by grace, offering by offering". That is what they did and have done.

Layer after layer of giving is shovelled away to reveal new ways of giving. And slowly the strata of the heart are uncovered with each new answer to God's "Forth and abroad!" to show, not buried ruins, but buried beauties of God's radical plan, the primal evidence of happiness being the total donation of the heart returned to him who fashioned and made it, to whom it alone belongs.

The dear bishop with whom God gifted us as father founder of our newest daughterhouse had sent two of his priests the long miles to Roswell, that they might study how the new Poor Clare monastery could best resemble the mother monastery down New Mexico way. They came. They studied. They returned to mid-country full of ideas for the future monastery and, more immediately, to redesigning the former convent given for our initial dwelling into a mini-monastery before our arrival. With benign understanding and arduous labor, they and many lay helpers had persuaded the little convent to look as much like a monastery as possible and particularly like a loved monastery in Roswell. Their persuasions were touchingly successful.

Yet there remained many new things to learn in an ancient way of life lived now in a new situation. One of these included the system of door locks. During the first weeks in our home, we felt we had mastered this new branch of learning. Only the portress did succeed in locking herself out from the cloister to the great world outside. The rest of us were at the far other end of our admittedly small domain occupied with new foundation activities unfavorable to perfect acoustics for things other. The locked-out portress made her desire to come in clear with repeated loud poundings on the door, but the poundings were not able to enter the ear canals of sisters engaged in hammering nails into walls, encouraging sewing machines to attain hitherto unrealized numerals on their speedometers, and other such and sundry highly audible enterprises. The portress grew desperate. She studied the one and only not-fence-but-real-wall that separated our little property from that of neighboring folk. It was of a short length but yet a tall wall. Having been taught in her youth by her two brothers the essential skills of mankind, such as climbing trees, she recalled her former expertise. Recalled it into physical action. She clambered up the wall and dropped down into the enclosure, safe and sound. But we wondered afterward if any or how many of our neighbors had observed her. We trusted that it was clear to any possible spectators of her wall-climbing that she was intent on leaping *in*, not out.

The Oblate Fathers showered goodness upon us in our modest beginning, as they were likewise to do when our permanent monastery began to rise on the grounds they had sold to us for $0,000,000.00. When at length the hour struck for beginning construction on the permanent monastery, God also gifted us with two remarkable artist-architects who designed the Poor Clare cloister-to-be with complete understanding of our desire for it and our dream of it. It was to be in the shape of a round world crowned with a cross. Friends would come to worship in the circle; we would dwell in the cross. And from the cross we would be about our loved business of gathering the whole round world into the arms of our life of prayer and penance.

From the beginning, the new foundation had been the spiritual property of Our Lady of Guadalupe. We explained to our long-suffering contractor that the new monastery absolutely and assuredly must be finished and dedicated before her December 12 solemnity. He, in turn, explained to us the impossibility of that early date. We smiled. He enlarged on his explanation. We smiled again and thought to encourage him by telling him how St. Teresa of Avila had once built a monastery in twelve days. His face remained impassive. We prayed. Then, he did it.

And when the business folk who must attend to such matters realized they must exercise their responsibility to make us knowledgeable about payments being due monthly, we reassured them. "Oh, we'll pay as long as we have any money." Somehow there always was just enough but never a smidgeon more than just enough money to meet each payment. Faith in God's Providence always just and barely supplied. Some good folk of the business world grew enthusiastic about having fund-raising drives. I explained that this was not our Poor Clare style. I reassured these eager friends that faith would always be vindicated. The monastery would be built and paid for. Faith would achieve it. I rejoiced that I had succeeded in convincing at least one intent financier when another intent financier incredulous at the veto on fund-raising campaigns inquired of the first intent financier: "How in the hell does she think we are going to build this monastery?" and received from him the explanation of one word spoken with impressive tonelessness: "Faith."

And so, on December 8, 1989, the Monastery of Our Lady of Mercy (as whom Our Lady of Guadalupe had described herself to her 1517 messenger, Blessed Juan Diego, saying: "I am a Merciful Mother") was indeed dedicated. The bishop of Roswell (Las Cruces) and the bishops or vicars of our earlier foundations came for the occasion. Scores of priests came, among them the beloved founder of the world-famous Shrine of Our Lady of the Snows, Father Edwin Guild, O.M.I. He had built a new Lourdes in the American Midwest. There was a large and thriving community of Oblate priests like himself there. Pilgrims came from all over the United States to this Shrine, the materialized dream of his heart and soul. But one thing had been long lacking. "Father Pop", as the young priests affectionately called Father Guild, had always wanted a cloister there, too. Frail now, and uncertain in his gait, he leaned on my arm as we walked toward the dedication. And we had a three-sentence interchange that I shall hold to my heart forever. It went like this:

FATHER POP: All these years I have prayed for clois-
    tered nuns to come.
MOTHER MARY FRANCIS: And now we are here.
FATHER POP: Yes, now you are here.

One could hardly burden this dialogue with further words.

It was a shaft of light turned upon the buried city of God's dear design brought into view at the price of hard shovelling away of nostalgia, of demur at another "Forth and abroad". It was a new glimpse of a beautiful city below.

For the glimpse to broaden into clearer viewing, there was required a spiritual expression of the material "making way" we have ruefully discovered to be absolutely necessary at regular intervals in order to "keep our lives uncluttered and our holdings small", as our Constitutions urge us (art. 53, no. 2). Nuns tend to be collectors. It is not a matter of desiring continually to enlarge our holdings but a deep-down and somewhat haunting fear that to discard anything is to run high risk of losing track of something that just might be just the thing we just could need someday. Related to this is the phenomenon of Poor Clares committed to the most profound realities of life and after-life drawing back from facing the reality that anything could ever be really worn out. Finished. Its life's course ended.

To dwell in a very small cell (monastic language for one's boudoir) is all well and good and happily accepted as such. The straw sack spread out its noble length on three boards is sufficient for repose. The little stand, the bench, the few shelves offer furnishings complete. The window supplying one's private patch of earth and sky view is luxury enough. And thus it is for all of the monastery. A little well supplies. But then, accumulation appears as a factor to be reckoned with or, more often, a temptation hardly to be resisted. The fascinating consideration about this accumulative drive is that it has nothing whatever to do with gathering easements or comforts or gadgets. It concerns rather a profound conviction that nothing can pass into totally verifiable uselessness or claim right of demise.

Here is something we do not need now and probably never shall. Only, maybe we might. There is this once fine specimen now broken and worn beyond possibility of repair or resuscitation, but it yet might be good for something someday in some circumstance. Here again is evidence of what has manifestly run its earthly course and clearly qualifies as undebatable material for the incinerator alone. Yet, we cannot, just cannot bring ourselves to dispose of these things.

A personal foray into a side section of the Roswell monastery basement some years ago yielded me memorable factual data on these above-described phenomena. I found some unrelated parts of a sewing machine that was perhaps used by Mrs. Noah on the Ark before the related parts got eddied into the flood waters. There was what I conjectured might have been the first pressure-cooker ever made. It had no lid. The one it must initially have boasted was likely on display in some museum somewhere. Several dozens of boxes neatly stacked on valuable shelf-space proved to hold garden shoes impressive by reason of boasting now only worn-down partial rubber soles without any other aids to locomotion such as straps, cuffs, or ties. All this and more left me with thoughts too deep for words but not for action.

There seems always this haunting fear that any or all of these collectors' items might someday be useful for something admittedly at present beyond the powers of human imagination. And so, in order to avoid having eventually to enlarge the monastery so that it might contain all these treasures that just might be useful someday for something, we initiated "make way days". Now and again, after a meaningfully grim announcement from the abbess, each sister looks through all her small earthly effects and her charges with a view to further reductions should her conscientious research yield no least evidence that the broken door hinge or the torn piece of wire fencing or the ballpoint pens that have lost all ability to convey a message to paper can claim any least right to enlargement of our monastic holdings. Clear directions will have been given by the abbess as to how to get to the incinerator and its adjunctive containers that await city public service. It can be done. Not without pain, for nuns are notoriously fearful of discarding anything that might yet reveal some latent usefulness if only, perhaps, fifty years hence.

Each life holds its own particularly memorable moments. Vivid in my memory is the face of our doctor at the historic moment when I proposed a question for his knowledgeable answering. A nurse friend had got us this medicine. A very mild sedative. Only none of us takes sedatives. I put my query to the doctor: "How long is this medicine ef-

fective? I mean, how long can we keep it?" I wanted to know for, in true nuns' style, I was holding
to our usual conviction that anything might be useful for something sometime. "How long have you
had it?" doctor asked, pleasantly enough. I pondered the passage of time and rendered my mea-
suring of it. "I think, about thirty years", I concluded. Doctor is a tall man in any circumstance.
At that moment, he seemed to grow before my
gaze into a giant of twelve feet or so as he peered
down at me. "THROW IT AWAY!" he said in measured resounding syllables. His tone was impressive. His face was, as we say, a study.

Just as a new foundation calls for making way in
our spiritual priorities, so does all contemplative,
even all Christian, living demand that we continually make way interiorly. What is our priority in
the spiritual life, whether inside or outside a cloister? Surely it is to attend on and serve God's will
in ungrudging love. Indeed, to do his will as a very
expression of love. Uniquely enough does a new
foundation elicit the heart's affirmation that "God
is enough, God is enough, and everything else is
not enough."

Do we not at times hear in our souls the voice of
God calling us "Forth and abroad" from accumu-
lations of mind and memory, from things stored
up in the heart that so weigh us down spiritually as

to preclude our making those new spiritual foundations which each one is called to make throughout life? Better, perhaps, to call them renovations, those new beginnings that must needs mark every spiritual life. Leaving in great pain of the heart one's mother monastery requires a certain parting from all one has come to love most, though one indeed discovers later that all these heart-wrenching sacrifices made in order to respond to God's "Forth and abroad!" are given back by him in full measure, pressed down and running over, as foundresses and foundation-allowing persons come to understand how nothing deep and beautiful can ever really be taken from the heart. It requires only that one desire to keep it.

It is vastly different with the lifelong patterns of interior renovations. They require a forgoing of the unbeautiful so that beauty may take possession, of nurtured untruths so that truth instead may be nourished, of all that defaces and cripples goodness so that goodness may be in command.

Who does not need periodically to make way in the memory where we may be harboring the "names of streets and numbers of the houses" (as the late Father Thomas Merton, O.C.S.O., once put it) where we have been hurt, misunderstood, rebuffed. It would hardly serve a soldier's mental health and peace of heart to rehearse at frequent intervals the way he felt when the shrapnel tore his limb. Yet, we can tend to do exactly that with the shrapnel that has torn the heart. It is indeed a curious paradox that we sometimes find it so difficult to make way in the memory by tossing into the spiritual incinerator what blocks the rising of new spiritual foundations, by tossing out the records that play old hurts with a stuck needle so that we cannot clearly hear God's "Forth and abroad!" to a fresh foundation of his love in our hearts.

The beautiful city that is God's creation of each one of us requires not only ongoing spiritual excavations of all that continually threatens to overlay and conceal basic individual truth and goodness but also a lifelong making-way—which is to say, making-*a*way—of what crowds the memory and bruises the soul. Materially, there is something endearing about nuns hoarding up permanently disabled household appliances lest these might someday reveal somehow some use yet upon the earth. Spiritually, it is, instead, devastating and destructive to retain in memory what distorts the spirit. A broken light fixture could perhaps yet be mended or at least used for a paperweight. A fracturing resentment or a moldering hurt "kept in good repair" will be useful only for introducing a life-threatening plague into the beautiful city of our humanity.

It needs human determination added to reliable divine grace for the tides of self-pity that can so successfully pollute the rivers of grace in the heart to be held back. Again, one does curious things sometimes in the spiritual life. God calls out, "Forth and abroad!" and offers us a raft. We sometimes prefer to drown in turgid waters.

In our newest foundation, the things spiritually relearned and more profoundly understood in a new beginning seemed to take on shape and substance in that Dedication Mass of 1989. The long, long lines of white-albed priests in procession that spoke somehow of the heavenly Jerusalem, the bishops anointing the face of the new altar with blessed oil, the little organ making a good case of its pretense at being a pipe organ for a day, the contractor singing the Mass parts along with us in the manner of a man bemused that, yes, he actually had got this building into a standing position, complete with walls and under roof, sooner than had been thought humanly possible, all of these and more proclaimed that God's "Forth and abroad!" had begot another new foundation for the glory of his name.

Yes, it was all glorious. But we remembered the private dedication day we had had months before when we had ventured, one Sunday morning, duly chaperoned with episcopal permission and guardianship into the half-finished building and followed the ritual of our hearts. We had wandered bemusedly through the unfinished rooms and marked off future individual cells. We had given first fulfillment to the ambition of the one very large room to be some day a chapel and nuns' choir by initiating the ancient choral chants of the Divine Office right then and there. Building temporary choir stalls was simple. We had only to turn the absent workmen's large emptied paint pails upside down and—*voila!* —a throne of prayer for each! We chanted and we sang and we marvelled. Then we went to the unfinished refectory and spread out our lunch on some boards standing handily by. All was dedicated. Especially our hearts. And now we could rest forever in the Amen! of this final "Forth and abroad".

At that point, only God heard the soft roll of drums and saw the garlanded carriages bearing other Roswell nuns into a charming village in a faraway land.

Chapter V

The Heart Has a
Mind of Its Own

"Forth and abroad!" That call of God continues to sound daily in the hearts of all who listen. There is the "Forth and abroad!" from the earthly tents we can tend to go on pitching in our hearts, our souls, even as with our lips we agree with the Apostle that, "We have not here a lasting city" (Heb 13:14). Is it not, in fact, an enlightenment of the Holy Spirit that we come to discover with a dismay hopefully enlivened with a certain amusement that we have within us a whole colony of tents? One could perhaps even say that one great work of the spiritual life is to fold one tent after another until at last God may discover within us only open space for his purposes.

But, too, there sounds sometimes that dramatic call to go forth from what is good, precious, prized, cherished, most beloved. To go abroad into a strange land for the sole and simple reason that God has sent out a summons. Privately within ourselves or communally by visible action, we determine our option: to respond or not to respond.

And so there sounded another call from God to our community here in a small and largely unknown city of our country while we were as usual happily occupied in our prayer, tending our garden, sweeping our halls, singingly content to be hidden away with God and with one another in our plain little farmhouse monastery. "Holland!" It was obviously impossible for us to consider a foundation in Holland. Our youngest daughterhouse of 1986 not yet three years old, our hearts not healed from the partings with sisters for our oldest daughterhouse in 1971. There was a by-and-large lack of years in the sisters for such an enterprise. Besides that, we don't know the Dutch language, the Dutch culture, the situation. We are clearly not equipped for reinitiating the life of St. Clare in a land where its continuance seems in question in many quarters. It was a clear folio we could present to God for his review. But he only repeated: "Holland!" That meant there was obviously a release from any process of "pre-discernment". God says: "Forth and abroad!" Our minds reply: "Impossible. At least, not now. This is all too precipitous." Our hearts reply: "How true. But—here we come." And after a while we begin to smile through our tears, noting once more that God is surely full of ideas and that he sometimes speaks to the heart what the mind cannot endorse.

Thus, on February 26, 1989, in the dark of night as once our Mother St. Clare set out in the dark of night to begin our Order, I set out with Sister Therese, superior of our youngest U.S. foundation, for Holland via Rome. The heart had insisted: "Go and see." Mind grudgingly agreed. So, there we were, in Lent, crossing the ocean in darkness on a crowded plane, alternately shiveringly cold and miserably hot, quite wanting in privacy, but coming to a certain happy realization that we are likely the only ones on this plane praying the canonical hours of the breviary (and yes, even softly singing its hymns together, head pressed against head) and a deepening understanding that we are never "out of our element" when our element is God. We began to laugh, a little ruefully, a little delightedly. We thought back a bit to the several hours we had remained grounded at Kennedy airport while the plane was de-iced only to need another de-icing after having had to wait longer for take-off because of the blinding snow. Meanwhile, God was de-icing our hearts, however much the snow of another parting threatened to blind our tremulous resolve.

There were glorious dramatic moments amid the scarcely poetic strangeness of it all. After the long, sleepless night came the dawn, Brother Sun slowly furthering his work of silvering the Atlantic Ocean and illuminating the spreading sky. We knew it was just precisely the time to pray the morning Office of Lauds. Then the captain gave a kind of roar, so dramatic his voice: "*Roma!*" And some minutes later: "We are now descending into Rome."

We knew, of course, exactly what we should do. We sang softly together, but at hearts' top volume: "You are Peter, and upon this rock I will build my Church." Our "Thanks be to God!" as the plane dropped its landing gear with a mighty thump on the airstrip of Rome reached back to the Little Sisters of the Poor who had supplied a rescue team for two small Poor Clare pilgrims the night before, threading us through the maze of Kennedy airport, making sure we did not board the plane for Egypt, which the press of the crowd around us offered as a ready possibility, fortifying us with warm sisterly embraces. We thankfully remembered the earlier airport official back in the United States who had solved the airline problem of overbooking on the economy class by putting us on first class. Our memory played back his studying our tourist-class tickets, peering at us again, flicking his eyes over our religious habits and saying: "Sisters, we are putting you on 'first class'", thus giving us our first encounter with the amenities of the kind of coach we had never experienced before and renewing our wonder as to the whereabouts of these lay-folk to whom the religious habit is said (by whom?) to be "a barrier".

More than a little dazed, we found ourselves in the huge press of the Fiumicino airport of Rome, Italian voices all around us, ourselves totally unsure of what to do next. But then arose before us the presence of Holy Church in the person of Augustine Cardinal Mayer. All was well. All was now very well indeed. We swung out into the sunlight where the waiting car would soon bring before our eyes the vision of that most beloved of enclosure walls, the "Vatican Wall", and the first sight of the parish church of us all: St. Peter's Basilica.

It had seemed an obvious conclusion that, if God should be summoning us forth and abroad out of little Roswell into a far-off strange country, we had a pressing need: the blessing of his vicar on earth. It was decidedly necessary that our enplanement for Holland touch down on the heart of the Church, that any possible selection of a city in which to root our Poor Clare lives anew in a foreign country must be one of vision clarified in the Eternal City. And so, God arranged, with a bit of human assistance, that Sister Therese and I be gathered into the heart of the Church at a Mass with our Holy Father in his exquisite tiny *capella privata*. One waits on the great stone steps outside, is scrutinized and admitted inside, crosses the Court of St. Damasus in the freshness of early morning, a softly tinted sky above, vividly uniformed Swiss Guards on duty. And then up stairs and stairs and stairs and into an elevator to emerge into a very large vestibule, there to meet a smiling secretary, Monsignor Stanislaw, who says warmly: "The Sisters from the United States?" And so the two little Sisters from the United States are ushered along with a group of Mexican bishops on their *ad limina* visit to the small chapel where our Holy Father is already kneeling at his prie-dieu before the altar. The white-robed figure, head in hands, is obviously rapt in deep prayer. "*Ecce, homo!*"—the silent words welled up in my heart: Behold, the one who is vicar of Christ on earth; behold, the one to whom has been entrusted the keys of the kingdom; behold, the man who carries in his great heart the weight of the whole world. There is a deep, deep silence in the little chapel.

How beautiful it is to watch the vesting of the Holy Father for Mass. He stands sweetly motionless, while attendant priests vest him, as though upon entering into the renewal of the Sacrifice of Calvary, he is saying: "Do with me as you will."

The Holy Father faces forward with the tiny congregation during Mass, but when he turns at the different greetings during the liturgy, there is on his face a little smile that turns up one cheek. Then there was the great moment of Holy Communion, receiving Christ from the hands of Christ's vicar. After the Mass, he was unvested as slowly and impressively as at the vesting, returning to his priedieu for his private thanksgiving, after having intoned the "Salve, Regina" with happy gusto. All seemed so serene now, so happy. The dear head was no longer buried in his hands but serenely bent in prayer that I would hold to be the comforting of the Lord to his vicar. I wanted just to look and look at him. "*Ecce, homo!*" But a kindly smiling attendant gently urged me on my way to the very large room where the Holy Father afterward greets each one who has been at his private Mass. He looked well, pink-cheeked, and smiling.

We took what seemed to us obviously our proper place—at the end of the line encircling the room. And when the attendant secretary identified us to Pope John Paul II as "the nuns from the United States, the Poor Clares", I was able to tell our Holy Father that we were going to Holland that very afternoon in initial pre-response to the invitation that we make a new foundation there. Pope John Paul had me repeat this. Then he mused: "Holland!"

We were privileged to look deep into his eyes, hold
and kiss his hand, and hear him say: "I bless you."
New vigor flowed into us. We had now indeed
received the strength we had come to the Eternal
City to gather before going to Holland as we did
that same afternoon. Surely we had no further excuse to falter on our pilgrim way to the Netherlands, and still less because we were accompanied
by Cardinal Mayer himself, who made it possible
for us to communicate easily in the tongue of Holland, to come to some conclusions in Holland, to
make some tentative pre-decisions in Holland, to
reinforce our *"Adsumus!"* in Holland.

A pleasing and deeply significant thing was that
we never felt, while in Holland, that we were in
a foreign land. An at-homeness was experienced
with the friendly people, the heartily extended kind
services on all sides, the general courtesy. There
was, though, also evident a certain pall of sadness
over all, and this readily explicable with the continued closing of churches, the dispersal of aged
religious to nursing homes, the scarcity of priests.

We drove then from 's-Hertogenbosch to Eindhoven and the Monastery of Poor Clares there,
where we were given such warm and loving hospitality by the aging Dutch nuns struggling so
valiantly to continue their Poor Clare life. It was
altogether satisfactory to have the Cardinal right

there in the guest quarters of the monastery. He celebrated the conventual Mass, addressed the community, toured the cloister, visited with us a possible temporary monastery and gave excellent advice about its possibilities, put everyone at ease and established everyone in joy by that atmosphere he creates and sustains around himself. The nuns, initially somewhat overcome at having the great Cardinal in their midst, said to me after his departure, "He is just so sweet and kind." I was deeply moved by this new witness of what it is that touches human hearts. Impressive indeed is brilliance of mind, illustriousness of position, elegance of manner, and all the rest; but what most deeply impressed the Dutch nuns was that "He is just so sweet and kind."

The Dutch bishop's vicar general had aligned three possibilities for our possible first years in Holland, should we possibly decide to make the foundation (which he did give me to understand they were wanting happily "to take for granted!"). After seeing the first one, I knew there was no need to investigate beyond this initial stop, which was at a large convent vacated only four months before by teaching sisters no longer able to function for want of membership. A beautiful statue of our Immaculate Mother looked down on me from her place above the entrance. I think I could say: she looked down *at* me. For under her image was inscribed

the title: *Maria Stichting* (the Mary Foundation).
I could hardly fail to get the message. We found
inside a lovely little chapel with a sanctuary sufficient to serve as cloister choir for little poor ones
beginning their little poor lives anew. We counted
fourteen "cells", a large room flooded with sunlight that seemed to announce itself as combina-
tion chapter room/community room. I could see
a likely refectory space, a room adaptable for a parlor with enclosure separation. And much more. It
all seemed to unfold like a dream. And both dream-
like and sturdily realistic was His Eminence at my
side, making suggestions about the arrangements
of the outer and inner doors to suit our portress
needs, marking off where the nuns could be situated in the sanctuary with a dividing screen from
the public chapel, commenting on the warm attic
where we "could hang our clothes when it rains,
because it rains so much in Holland". We knew
that, if we were to go to Holland at all, it would
be to Maria Stichting in Elshout Village that we
would go. With minds unsure and hearts unsteady,
we went back home to Roswell.

But where is home on this stopping-off place of
earth en route to eternity?

The interior yearning in the human heart for that
great and final going forth and abroad into eternity
finds both a satisfaction and a dissatisfaction with

earth. So satisfying is earth in its multiple beauties and its heartshaking portents of the eternal life to come, so disappointing in its inability to sustain or quiet the aching outreach of the human spirit for that permanent home we have never seen but for which we suffer such an all-pervasive nostalgia. Earth is best earth when it touches most closely on eternity. It is a stunning paradox that it is those who are most appreciative of and intrigued by the beauties of earth who are least rooted in it, who are just "passing through". It is only when we strive to set up a lasting city on earth that we begin demanding of earth what it cannot give, that we become inimical to earth, angry at its inability to afford us permanent joy, to be a lasting city. One thinks of St. Francis of Assisi singing out his "Canticle of the Creatures" in sheer, joyous, grateful wonder for his mother earth, his sister the moon, his brother wind, and all the rest, while burning out his small person in yearning for eternity.

Francis was at home everywhere, whether at Rivo Torto, where he transformed a sort of hovel into a friars' dormitory by the simple expedient of marking off each one's narrow place with a chalk mark on the wall, or in the palace of Cardinal Hugolino, where, invited for dinner, Francis brought his own meager lunch lest he be feasting while other friars were fasting. We did not stop at

"Cardinal Hugolino's" on our way home to Roswell, but we did once stop at the Hilton Hotel. Let me tell you.

In Holland I had got a heavy cold when a sturdy Dutch cold germ decided to see what it could do with a sturdy American physique or lack of same. At a stop-over of several hours back on U.S. *terra firma*, we wondered whether there might be a place to rest in the airport. There was, although not precisely at the airport. Again, this full religious habit that has left some workshop folk hoarse from declaring it outmoded and distancing from forward-looking humanity drew instead good numbers of humanity to our side. Did we need something? Could they do anything? They were anxious. For I am one of those who, when gnawed on by a hungry cold-bug, look pretty well ready for burial.

Well, yes, we smiled between sneezes. If we could just rest a bit. And we did. In a room at the Hilton Hotel across the street from the airport, this quickly arranged and paid for by strangers for two nuns in need.

We entered the portals of Hilton's wide spaces, were given a key to "our room", were told that dinner would be brought to us, and all of this paid for by, no, not a stranger, for to daughters of St. Francis and St. Clare, no one on earth is a "stranger", but by our new-found friend whose name we did not know. We declined dinner, explaining that we had our lunch with us. Perhaps the first patrons ever to have brought their lunch along to the Hilton, we spread it out on the elegant small table in the luxurious room which had been arranged for us. I expect we made history there. For it seems unlikely that the Hilton had ever before been party to a "dinner" of some cheese that was sweating mightily from its long journeying and two bananas that had blackened from the duress of travel. We had some crackers, too, which showed themselves as better survivors. After thus feasting, we lay down to rest on a bed of size and density totally alien to Poor Clare straw sacks. Later, our new friend collected us, returned us to the airport, and bought us a box of chocolates to ward off further physical travail on the final flight home. One just wants to start praying for the ubiquitous folk who love recognizable nuns because they somehow divine that these nuns love them. Which we do.

When the very large transoceanic plane deposited us again on our native soil, we were transferred to the large U.S. plane in its turn to deliver us over to the very small plane that comes into Roswell and on which you are reminded by a friendly pilot to watch, no, not so much your step, but your head, as you make your hunched-over way in and out of this low-ceilinged mechanical bird. "Watch yor haid!" caroled the Southwestern voice. Heads intact, we sat ourselves down and settled, more or less, our fluttering hearts. And arrived once again in Roswell, we entered into a series of *cor unum* chapters.

So, what is a *cor unum* chapter?

It has to be true to its name: *cor unum*, one (in) heart, or it is better not held. The nuns assemble in one room, the chapter room, with as many ideas as there are nuns. But with a single heart. To be true and availing, healthfully variant cogitations and vigorously offered diverse opinions must be sustained in happy good health by a single community heart. Once a young nun informed her fellow sisters (and I pause there to ponder the reaction of the anti-exclusive-language militants to that term, while considering whether a substitute "person sisters" might be too novel for anyone save, ironically enough, the old-fashioned folk who have always been and who remain content in the company of mankind whose number and increase is possible only because of women) . . .

Return to text: said young nun informed her fellow sisters that she felt free to offer her emphatic opinions on points up for discussion and decision (those said opinions being frequently variant and always vigorous), because Mother Abbess would make the final decision. Free, for thus she would hold forth without fear of overpowering voices of lesser carrying power and more *calmo* expression. "I say just what I think," she beamed, pink from her just-delivered determinate opinion, "and Mother makes the definitive conclusion. We don't just take a head count." That alone would seem to suffice for throwing certain assemblies of divergent approach into a state of horror. It all depends on whether there is *cor unum in vocibus diversibus.* Or not.

We set ourselves to consider. And in the freedom of the ever-prevailing *cor unum*, which really translates simply as *community*, many thoughts arose from many minds:

1. We have a very young dependent new foundation. It is more than inopportune even to consider another new beginning at this point.

2. Our number is depleted from birthing foundations. Practicality precludes further subtraction now.

3. We are talking about a foreign country. We do not know the language, the culture, the customs. We are obviously unqualified.

4. This would be an unjustifiably rash decision.

Minds ticked off the sound reasons. Memory tabulated them. All was clear. We could only say: "Sorry about the situation, God; but you surely cannot expect us to do anything about it. We do regret and grieve that St. Clare's dream seems to be running short on dreamers. But we certainly cannot do anything about bolstering the numbers. We shall assuredly pray. But we have to be practical."

Things were going well. Minds were expressing clear conclusions. But then the *cor unum* of community showed once again that it had a mind of its own, as we went back over our points-well-taken by the mind:

1. We remembered that it had been scarcely opportune for an eighteen-year-old female Italian aristocrat named Clare Offreduccio to initiate for women a religious life such as had never been known, dreamed of, or nightmared before. Only, she did it.

2. St. Clare's first community numbered one: Clare. True enough, in a short time the number swelled to two when Clare's younger sister applied for admission and was accepted by big sister.

3. There was hardly a "country" more foreign to everyone in the world than the spiritual country into which St. Francis brought St. Clare. The language spoken was not of earth. The culture pertained to amenities of soul inexplicable to any who could not abandon themselves to a learning process reaching into the roots of soul as well as of heart.

4. But then, was not the most rash (by all human standards) decision ever taken that one God took: to save all of mankind by the ignominious human demise of his only begotten Son? And we found ourselves recalling how that dying of Christ was preceded by three years of his teaching such preposterous principles as offering your left cheek for new smiting when someone had slapped your right cheek, or going another mile with one who had already selfishly imposed a hard first mile on you, of finding cause for rejoicing when others had heaped all manner of cruelties upon you.

It was becoming uncomfortably clear that the *cor unum* of community was beginning to challenge the firm conclusions of sturdy reason. The manner and mode of our redemption was itself, we had to agree, quite "unreasonable". Preposterous, really. And so does the whole plan of salvation appear to a merely "reasonable" assessment. Together, our hearts set out on a new appraisal of salvation history, mankind's and our individual own. And we did take our minds along. For one must allow and even urge the mind to go as far as it can travel before one can really either appreciate its preciousness or confess its limitations.

Neither contemplative prayer itself nor life decisions would be well served by the discarding of one's God-given intellect or by its disuse. However true it is that the intellect must often lie still before the presence of the King and his amazing Deific proposals, it also remains true that neither preparation for praying better nor preparation for deciding better is well served by thinking less. Perhaps nowhere more than in the cloister must the intellect be finely honed to achieve its own full possibilities. But perhaps nowhere, too, more than in a life of contemplative prayer does the heart assert its own findings and often enough convert the mind to "cardiac conclusions". Contemplation cannot be diagrammed. But it naturally begets and nurtures a feeling for and expression of the good, the true, and the beautiful, and this not so much specific as generic. It reaches out into the mind's little and large decisions, which in the end issue from the heart.

The foundress of the Poor Clare nuns, St. Clare of Assisi, was a woman who quite noticeably and even notably used her mind. Just the fact of her being the first woman in history herself to write a Rule of Life for nuns indicates a mind well occupied with the proper business of a mind. The complementary fact that she trailed beauty after her, shed loveliness about her, took ladyhood as a continual manner of living gives evidence that her heart was in good partnership with her mind. It was the same with her father and mentor, St. Francis of Assisi, whose great mind was enlightened by God and used by himself to initiate a whole new way of religious life in the Church, while his heart made of him a poet, a singer, and sometimes a dancer, on occasion, while delivering his sermons.

There is an appalling dearth of thinking in our times even in the theological domain, where the strangest conclusions are sometimes drawn from the most tortured syllogisms. However, there is also what may be simply and accurately described as a lack of heart. When the powers of the mind have gone as far as they can go and concluded as much of truth as lies within their possibilities, then those powers must give humble heed to the heart. Is not, in fact, a humble mind one that has energetically exhausted all its potential in order to recognize its limitations? "All that I have written seems to me as a little straw", concluded St. Thomas Aquinas toward the end of his life. His humble assessment of himself and his works was accurate. For is not indeed everything that the mind can achieve really only "straw" before the greatness of God and his incredible designs? He is a God, however, who is glorified by our gathering all the "straw" we can for his service and the directing of our own free-willed lives, while vigorously routing any temptation toward torpor of intellect.

Yes, a mind is for using. Its sound conclusions call for the most serious pondering. And for the heart to claim absolute sovereignty whether over life itself or the decisions that make for life's unfolding pattern is clearly an unjustified and perilous assumption. Yet, for the mind to insist on its supreme authority in decision making, including the decision to disregard the evidence of the heart, is a counterinsistence fraught, if not always with peril, at least with frequent and sometimes very serious loss to the proprietors of mind and heart. Indeed, it is the mind that delivers to the will the evidence on which the will pronounces. Nonetheless, cerebral conclusions need enfleshing with what only the heart can contribute: the findings of love that can never, if the love is real and true, be at enmity with the mind but which can sometimes unseat the mind's best justified decisions or even topple them. The mind of the father of the prodigal son in the Gospel must surely have rendered the father completely just conclusions: the son must be penanced. He must make reparation. He must become practiced in contrition. He must come to assess himself as a thoroughgoing rotter. It's all for his own good, before there be any expression of such unduly swift and overly facile pardon as might leave the boy forever unaware of the heinousness of his crimes.

The father might well have then had it in mind to show welcome, once the son's state of soul had been made clear to him. It was good, clear thinking. But the father's heart got the better of any sound conclusions of reasonableness. He just held out his arms to his returned renegade son. And threw a party. This is Jesus' revelation of how the heavenly Father forgives, Jesus being the sole Person qualified to offer such a revelation, as the *Catechism of the Catholic Church* points out (no. 1439).

It is a most wondrous partnership, that of mind and heart. Needing to be established and maintained in every way of living, it has its particular significance in a cloister where minds are hopefully meeting others' minds all the time, where hearts are affected by other hearts on that same life schedule.

Applicants come. One is so shy that the parlor interview witnesses the girl's history-making slowness in advancing from the farthest corner of the parlor to the beckoning nearness of the parlor screen. The mind rightly wonders about her suitability for a life involving lots of sisters at very close range in a setting with no place for a loner. Only, the heart insists that there is more to be considered here. It could be awe and wonder at the possibility of being called by God to a rare and demanding vocation that gives pause to the mind, amazement to the heart, a halting of motion. Is she a person lacking in firm purpose? The mind in suspension wants to know, for it does wonder and hesitate. But it will never know if the heart does not enter the scene and let its love make possible the sorting out of the mind's proffered possibilities.

Another comes in her very short green skirt and bright red stockings, tossing her long black hair on her shoulders with every animated movement. She has a thousand questions. And the mind takes pause at such a double portion of animation breaking out in every movement and word. Will this intense little person be able to survive the quietude of a cloister, the soul-repose of the contemplative life? Then the heart sends out a reassuring directive. It remembers a very great contemplative and some of her more amazing Gospel-recorded positionings and statements. After Joseph of Arimathaea had laid the Body of Jesus in a new tomb and rolled a huge stone against it, we are told (Mt 27:59–61), Mary Magdalen positioned herself facing the tomb and the stone that doubtless she planned on rolling away personally if other help were wanting. Entirely inconsiderate of its heft. "I will take him away!" (Jn 20:15). How? Where? To St. Mary Magdalen, those would be later considerations.

Joint observations and conclusions of mind and

heart in good partnership can make possible a believing and nurturing life-formation for two potential contemplative Poor Clares.

And so, little by little, at our *cor unum* chapters thematic of a possible foundation in the Netherlands, hearts and minds came into partnership. "If we don't go, how do we explain this to God?" Do we say, "Frightfully sorry, God, but . . ." It does trail off. What do we say to St. Francis our father? "It really is totally impracticable?" Only, Francis never included "impracticable" in his cognitive tool kit. And to St. Clare? What? "We feel really distressed that your Order is thinning out so sadly. Do know how much we regret it, even though we cannot, of course, ourselves do anything about it." It can, at such turns of the road, be a frightening thing to look into the eyes of St. Clare, to meet her unwavering gaze.

As we faltered ever most observably in our initial negative reaction, the *cor unum* chapters were getting more *cor* and less *mens practica* at each session. "It's amazing how much the Dutch people know 'by heart'", I commented, if only to float some air into the discussion. "They sing all the Gregorian Chant Ordinaries by heart. After the Lenten Masses we attended, the lay congregation sang the entire five verses of 'Attende, Domine, et Miserere' by heart." Everyone was properly impressed by this piece of information. "But there are so many sad faces, especially of priests", I added.

Just then a prophet, if she did not rise up, at least spoke up. "Maybe we ought to go to help them smile." That was the moment. It was such a solidly Franciscan and Franciscanly solid reason. One small Assisian had made a whole world smile again. And we find it still generally smiling in the memory of his presence. Here was something within our compass. We were all *cor unum* about that. We know how to smile, if not how to speak Dutch. And, in the end, we all know (as in the beginning, too) that a smile is more basic communication than a word. So, all right. We would go to Holland and found a new community. And the prophet was to be one of those to go.

Minds had contributed to our considerations and would hopefully continue at their appointed task. But it was a clear victory for hearts. A community heart. *Cor unum.*

Chapter VI

Across the Sea

O blessed Jesus,
I dedicate myself in health, in illness,
in my life, in my death,
IN ALL MY DESIRES, IN ALL MY DEEDS,
so that I may never work henceforth
except for your glory, for the salvation of souls,
and for that for which you have chosen me.
FROM THIS MOMENT ON, DEAREST LORD,
THERE IS NOTHING I AM NOT PREPARED
TO UNDERTAKE FOR LOVE OF YOU.

— *St. Colette of Corbie*

Back in the early fifteenth century, the future St. Colette was very happy in her little Franciscan anchorhold in Corbie, France. She had disappeared into God, offering her young life as a hidden sacrifice of prayer and joyous penitence to God for his glory and for the salvation of souls. It was clearly his plan for her. She rejoiced in it. She seems not to have taken into account, however, that God's plan has a way of unfolding. And unfolding . . . She put up a notably sturdy resistance to that unfolding when God asked of her to disappear into himself in a quite different way from what she could ever have anticipated. It was made clear to her that she was to spend her life restoring the Primitive Rule of St. Clare where it had drifted and lapsed into the primitiveness of fallen human nature seeking an easier game while preserving the name, where rule had come to pertain to the despotism of self-pandering ease. It was only after a struggle of her heart and her soul "unto death" that she was able to offer herself anew to God in her prayer of dedication given there above. She had been contentedly prepared to be hiddenly his. Now, bowed down before his will and his grace, she vowed that there was *nothing* she was not prepared to undertake for love of him. And that unfolding will of his was to take her on long and arduous journeyings, making one Poor Clare foundation after another, and spending her years and her strength till the end of her long earthly life in going from one of these foundations to another, always encouraging, always newly imposing Love's sweet demands, always laboring to evoke a full and radical response from her ever-multiplying spiritual daughters, as she labored ever to evoke it from herself.

The story of St. Colette's remarkable life we have gathered and translated from multiple ancient manuscripts and documents and set into book form: *Walled in Light*. We could not have dreamed that in our own small way we would be invited by God to follow her out of, no, not an anchorhold, but out of our own dearly loved cloister into a faraway land. Her prayer of dedication we have been invited in our little measure to make our own.

We have had to expand *"all our desires"* beyond assuredly remaining after four foundations, all of us happily and now henceforth forever together in Roswell, to further boundaries of God's desires. We had been so content striving *"in all our deeds"* of prayer and humble labors and sisterhood right here, all together; but then it became dramatically and unmistakably clear that there were other deeds to be done, the deeds of transporting these same loved deeds into another place. And in 1990 we had our struggle, too, "unto the death of the heart" of each of us, in enlarging the *"nothing we are not prepared to undertake for love of God"* to include the physical parting with yet six more cherished sisters for a land across the sea. So, on March 8, 1990, the beloved six pioneers, their abbess, and the superior of our youngest U.S. foundation were herded, not into a covered wagon, as was St. Colette's mode of travel with young foundresses in tow, but into the plane that was to take us to Holland and another new beginning.

What finalizes the assemblage of those who go forth and abroad? What precedes the definitive roster? Prayer and pain. It has never been our foundation methodology for the abbess simply to look over the flock, make decisions, summon some folk forward out of the parent sheepfold, and say: "Go. I have decided that you will be a foundress." For it is a much more profound decision-making than counting off six "sparables", a decision rendered both initially and terminally impossible by reason of our having no sisters to spare. Each nun is unique, irreplaceable, indispensable. Nor is it a case of half a dozen or more hearts thundering with joy at the possibility of setting out for new shores. That no one wants of herself to go anywhere farther than the vegetable field at 809 E. 19th Street, Roswell, is the true indispensable for a Godly going forth.

Oh, indeed, we all of us want to dot the world map with ever-multiplying cloisters where the business of worship in total surrender to God and service of all his people from within "the King's rooms" is one's life work by night and by day. Only, no one wants to go anywhere. Particularly not if all of the other sisters are not going along.

So, we discern the membership of a new foundation less in weighing out persons and possibilities than in suffering and trusting prayer that is, of course, not unaccompanied by long, deep pondering. Only after that does the abbess deliver her findings, one by one, to the sisters who have emerged from the prayer and the pondering. The emergents then take to prayer (and in shock) their initial certainty that, oh, no, they are not the ones. Only after a while it becomes clear that what God has spoken in the heart of the abbess has been likewise spoken in the hearts of the foundresses-to-be. If it has not been, then further prayer and ponderings are in order. God has to be heard saying the same thing to both abbess and sisters.

There was, if possible, an even more profound aching silence in the monastery when the names of the Holland foundresses were made known. It was on the transferred Solemnity of the Annunciation, April 3, 1989, that I announced their names. The monastery was wrapped in silence all the day after that early morning chapter assembly. It seemed that we all somehow huddled together at the Divine Office, in the refectory. And the regular period of evening recreation was another huddling together in a deepened understanding of sisterhood. The world is so full of people wanting only to get away from one another. Surely God is glorified by the tears of those who can scarcely bear the prospect of another parting from one another. In that we find our comfort.

True, after any new foundation the going and the remaining visually see one another no more. Still, there is something much more comfortable for mind and heart in knowing that we are, after all, only perhaps half a dozen States of the U.S. apart. It gives a kind of "just down the street" feeling that is very comforting and sets well on the spiritual reality of profound inseparability. That ocean seems to make a difference. Across the ocean! We knew that we had to reduce that impossible mileage at once before it got, if not the upper hand, surely the upper heart. So, we *all* began learning Dutch. In no time the community was praying aloud our daily rosary in what was undoubtedly the most remarkable Nederlands yet heard on the earth. But for what was wanting in the pronunciation there was purposeful sisterly love to supply.

And then the day came for eight of us to take to the skies again.

Our loved Little Sisters of the Poor were again at the airport in New York to shepherd us along and bolster our courage those last minutes on native soil when it tended to flag into a "Let's just turn around and go back to Roswell!" We learned, ruefully, of the unique mode of "disappearing" into God which is to disappear into a long night over an ocean we could not see, stiffly crowded into narrow seats, but happily crowded against one another. Again there was strength and comfort and "home" in praying our Divine Office. What an anchor for a largely confused body (what time is it, anyhow?) and a puzzled spirit (where is the community? why doesn't the bell ring?) is the breviary! The canonical hours, interspersed with the rosary, bore us up on stouter, surer wings than the vast-spreading wings of the huge plane.

In all the strangeness of our surroundings we yet managed to exercise an energetic concern for Poor Clare domestic needs of the future. The stewardess came along, proffering a substantial "snack" that we chose to waive in favor of our Poor Clare lunch boxes from "home". But then I noticed that the snack boasted a beverage notable by its absence from our homemade lunches. There was a small bottle of wine with each serving.

Now, it is an immemorial monastic custom through all the centuries that the ceremonial dinner on Holy Thursday include a little serving of wine for each sister in memory of the Last Supper and of the wine that was made by Christ Jesus into his own Precious Blood. Here we were, above the Atlantic Ocean midway between New York and Amsterdam and midway in Lent. Holy Week was becoming imminent. Holy Thursday in a new monastery in a new land would shortly be upon us. And our effects included no wine for that all-meaningful and sacred ceremonial dinner. My heart gave a leap. My mind dialed to: "P" . . . *p*racticality, *p*reparation. I expect my eyes lit up so that it was a shining-eyed abbess who undoubtedly gave the stewardess material for long pondering after recovery from shock. "No," I smiled, "we have our own lunch." Then I enthusiastically confided: "But we would like to have all those little bottles of wine." With something of a "Well, one never knows" expression, the stewardess politely if somewhat dazedly handed us each a little bottle of wine.

I turned to the other sisters behind me and across the aisle and hastily hissed away their disbelief with a meaningful: "Everyone take the wine!" in my best abbatial issuance of high command. Everyone took it in bemused silence, save for our Belgian-born member, who has a way of lapsing into her native French at historic and dramatic moments. "*Mon Dieu!*" she whispered incredulously as she obediently reached for the wine. One foundress, with an expression of, "I regret that I have but one life to give for obedience", set about drinking her wine, a pursuit almost immediately terminated as

I whispered: "No! No! It's for Holy Thursday!" It remained then only to pack all eight little bottles into one sister's carry-on, a feat she watched with something of the dismal countenance that can gather from the prospect of being the nun who got off the plane with audible clinking sounds coming from her carry-on, dropped same, and filled the airport with the "odor of her ointments". However, obedient to the end, she accepted her assignment as her personal items from the carry-on were parceled out to the other sisters not chosen for her noble task. But God was with his people. His obedient daughter maintained her grip upon the carry-on. And we had our ceremonial wine for the approaching Holy Thursday. We could feel, therefore, somewhat situated for the future.

And then, at last, it was morning, with a silvery ocean made visible by a brilliant orange sun. The great bird of the plane alighted in Rome, the "home town" of all Catholics. We flexed our aching muscles and tuned up our tired spirits in the wonder of being home indeed. For this is where our Pastor lives, our beloved Holy Father. This is our parish.

Lost in the huge Fiumicino airport in Rome, we had somehow got ourselves into the wrong assemblage and were aligned with those enplaning for Athens, Greece. Happily, we were rescued by the sight of a loved familiar figure, His Eminence, Augustine Mayer. He and two of his staff were there to meet and assist us. We remembered our Mother St. Clare and Cardinal Hugolino and a number of other "family traditions". We recalled most of all the solicitude of our Mother the Church for her least daughters.

Our curious luggage of assorted cardboard boxes and suitcases of advanced age were collected at last, and we were taken to the Generalate of the Sisters of the Sorrowful Mother, who gave hospitality to us little country folk as though we had been queens. We were to remain in their gracious company until the early morning take-off for Holland some few days later. This time was to allow for the wondrous privilege of being, eight strong (or perhaps more accurately: eight-strengthened) at a private Mass with our Holy Father and meeting with His Eminence, Joseph Cardinal Ratzinger, and His Eminence, Jean Jerome Cardinal Hamer. One can hardly begin a new foundation in a foreign land without the blessing of the Supreme Pontiff, can one? Obviously not. One needs to be strengthened by the blessing and encouragement of the Prefect of the Congregation for the Doctrine of the Faith, that we each and all may keep faith with our vocation, our Clare-given charism in a new beginning. Not so? And one must be warmed by the paternal geniality of the Prefect of the Congregation for Institutes of the Consecrated Life if the folk of a new foundation are to remain firm in religious consecration in a new setting. Of course. These were great and solemn events, not without their touches of humor, as when an American subsecretary at the Congregation, after having greeted me as I awaited the Cardinal, then espied the whole group in another reception room and called out to any available ears: "Wow! There's a whole *gang* of them!"

The Mass with our Holy Father this time was in a larger chapel. There was an organ in the rear, not to be summoned into any musical outpouring that day, but with its bench offering seating accommodations for two more in the crowded chapel. Two Poor Clares. Ever since that day and even now one of them modestly recalls to anyone who has not heard it before or even to those who have, "We were at Mass with the Holy Father, and I was at the organ."

Pope John Paul II looked an older, wearier, and more anguished shepherd than in the previous year. Small wonder. He entered the chapel already vested and with mitre and crozier. He sat to the side of the sanctuary, facing us, during the first part of the liturgy, most of the time with his eyes closed, but occasionally turning his gaze slowly over his little congregation. I recall how many different bishops and

Fathers Provincial have told us of that penetrating glance turned on them and how they felt that each was "known and seen, through and through" by that Supreme Shepherd of souls. We experienced that, too. It made us happy. For we felt that our Holy Father would thus know how totally we love him and with what complete loyalty. One experiences in one's own small measure the nearly overwhelming universal ecclesial burden that weighs upon the heart of Pope John Paul II. But one seems to experience also, really to "see" with the eyes of the soul, how our Lord comforts his vicar on earth. For after the Mass, in the audience hall, the Holy Father was relaxed and smiling. He had once more called God down upon the altar at Mass; it seemed manifest that God newly present was now quickening his vicar's step, easing the care from his face and his heart.

We were overwhelmed at his Holiness' leisurely lingering with our little group of eight, spread out in one line "from end to end" before him. Each sister felt that big, strong hand laid on her head or felt the sign of the Cross traced on her forehead. The Holy Father was smiling and remarking contentedly: "Good Sisters! Good Sisters!" Indeed we do so want to be and were newly inspired to try to be.

Our Holy Father asked where in Holland we

were making the foundation. When we replied: "Diocese of 's-Hertogenbosch", His Holiness immediately said: "Bishop ter Schure! ter Schure!" That the Pope can so immediately identify our bishop out of the thousands of bishops was an amazing joy, and one I was to be so happy to communicate to Bishop ter Schure later in Holland. When he had reached the end of our little line, Pope John Paul returned to the line's center, extended his hand, pointed his finger, and said: "Go! Renew the Church." We shall never forget it. "*From this moment on . . .*" And how does one "renew the Church"? Clearly, only from within one's own self-renewal in love and dedication.

Then came the morning of our departure from Rome, the last look at the great dome of St. Peter's by the soft clouds of just postdawn. We remembered the dear word of our youngest foundress: "Nothing is small at St. Peter's except Jesus." Yes, in the Blessed Sacrament chapel in the great basilica, praying our Office before the small Host in the tall monstrance, we could reflect that all the glory of this largest church in Christendom has meaning only because of him there present in that little Host. Everything so large . . . our same sage youngest suggested that there was plenty of room in St. Peter's Square for us to make a foundation right there, if the pigeons would just move over.

But for now it was: on to the airport, where it took more than a bit of doing to get eight Poor Clares and most of their earthly effects organized and enplaned. Then we were again swept up into the skies, and a great hush fell upon us. We were going to Holland, six of us to remain there.

The hush on our hearts lifted into a chorus of gratitude as we deplaned and saw so many waving hands. A whole little company of "official welcomers" was there to greet us and drive us to the Poor Clare Monastery in Eindhoven where we were to remain for three days, preparing for the dedication of our own mini-monastery in Elshout Village. Our sisters in Eindhoven were wondrously kind to us, looking after our needs until our great day came: March 17. Never could we have dreamed what the special "commission" set up to assist us, in company with our Bishop ter Schure, Vicaris Schroeder, the mayor, other notables, and the townsfolk, had prepared for us. Our arms were heaped with flowers as we left the monastery of Eindhoven to be driven to the outskirts of Elshout. Nothing at all had been divulged of what was to be. So, when we were invited to leave the little procession of cars, we were amazed to hear a band playing. And then the medieval pageantry began to unfold.

Round-eyed with wonder, we were taken to two

horse-drawn carts, four of us enthroned in each. Everyone else walked. There were two bands playing. Guildsmen of the *Onze Lieve Vrouwe Schuts* (the Guild of Our Lady of Protection—the title expresses Our Lady's guardianship) in their colorful uniforms marched beside us, before us, behind us. There was a children's corps holding raised batons and wearing smart plumed caps. They were to make a guard of honor for us as we entered the town hall, holding the batons in a processional arch, with each pair of batons lifted high as we passed through the archway. There were bridesmen leading the horses. And there was joy everywhere. The townspeople lined the streets, smiling and waving, some weeping. And, once in the town hall, there were welcomes and more welcomes— from the bishop, the vicar, the commission, the mayor, priests, religious, laity. I was asked to speak, too, with our special "guardian angel", Mr. Vincent Van den Donk, translating. Yet I felt that the dear people already understood what I was saying before it was repeated in their own language.

It was from Holland, I told the people, that our U.S. founding Mothers had come in 1877. Having been driven out of their native Germany by the Kulturkampf, the foundresses-for-America had been given sanctuary in Holland. Now, their Poor Clare daughters of a century and score of years later were coming to repay Holland's favor and seek its hospitality again, this time in a new foundation. I told them that I was entrusting to them six measures of my most precious treasure: spiritual daughters. And I saw that they understood. The American ambassador to Holland had sent a letter of regret that he, too, could not have been with us on this day of our dedication. But, somehow, we felt that all of our own native land was there with us. And . . . "*From this moment on . . .*" the two countries were to enjoy a new and lasting bond.

The band played for us again. The welcoming speeches continued. The smiles went on making their own arches of love over us. And then we were solemnly marched from the town hall to our own little monastery, Clarissenklooster Maria Moeder van de Kerk. But the celebration was not yet done! On the lawns before our monastery, two of the guildsmen performed their historic ancient flourishing of the colors. Enthralled, bemused, we watched the two costumed men furl and unfurl the huge flags, leap over the flags, dance under the flags, thrust the flags "up in the heavens", bring the flags down to the earth (but never once allowing the flags to touch the ground), while the drum roll went on and on, and the King and Queen of the Guild, costumed and crowned, stood with us to watch. Then the symbolic gifts of welcome were offered: sausage and bread. But Mr. Van den Donk explained that the symbolic sausage was substituted by symbolic fish, "because the Poor Clares do not ever eat meat!" Especially moving was the flower-lined entrance walk to our monastery, with its boxes of vari-colored blooms set on high white pedestals. And at the front sidewalk and again at the entrance door were erected large, large flags— the Dutch flag and the American flag. "*. . . From this moment on . . .*"

The brief period of "open house" featured flowers everywhere and smiling well-wishers everywhere. Then it was done, the cloister locked off and the first Office of Vespers chanted in our tiny choir, which reminded us so strongly and heart-shakingly of the like-proportioned choir at San Damiano in Assisi. Poor Clare life had begun anew in Elshout, Holland. "*From this moment on . . .*"

It was twilight then. We pulled our three donated refectory tables together in the soothing kindliness of the dusk, set up the few candles we had, and partook of our first repast in our new home by the light of the candles on the tables and those in our hearts. We were hushed with a wonder that, temporarily at least, drew a rainbow over the readily damp nostalgia of our hearts. Then the doorbell rang. It was an elderly man, and he bore a gift. A can of sardines. We knew that we had somehow then really arrived in Elshout.

And after a few days, THE CRATE came. It deserves solid capitalization, the crate from the United States that had still been reposing in customs at Rotterdam when we arrived. That crate with extremely important and, really, quite priceless items within it: the wooden tabernacle fashioned by priestly hands for the first temporary choir of our 1986 foundation and in which had traveled across the sea the figurine of the Infant Jesus for our temporary choir come Elshout's first Christmas, the standing pyx for the Blessed Sacrament from the first temporary monastery of our 1977 foundation, our metal monastic refectory dishes, our organ books, our cell crucifixes and holy water fonts, our image of Our Lady of Guadalupe, our sewing kits and aprons, our toolbox, our liturgical charts, and other similar Poor Clare treasures. We had been forewarned that THE CRATE would just be deposited in the drive, we and it henceforth left to our own devices. But we prayed and hoped. And we exhausted our entire and then very meager Dutch vocabulary on the driver. He politely heard us out. Then he said in good old American: "Okay! Where do you want it?" And he and his companion persuaded the nailed CRATE to disgorge all its boxes of Poor Clare treasures onto the walk, thence to be carried up to the second floor by himself and that same blessed companion. We were in business!

We went forward into the vital enterprise of exploring THE CRATE and extracting bits of Roswell daily life therefrom. Someone retrieved her ballpoint pen, the one that actually writes and, therefore, could not have been put at risk in less secure encasing than THE CRATE. The cook had a soup pot from Roswell's early and small-of-members days. The refectorian had found the little table bell that proclaims the meal's beginning and its end. The sacristan had a portion of incense for our Exposition of the Blessed Sacrament. We felt established. And that night at the Office of the Annunciation, our midnight rising for Matins began in Holland, we trust never to end. ". . . *From this moment on . . .*"

Important enterprises went forward. A roll of thin linoleum was discovered in the attic. Oh, what a find that was! One day was dedicated to getting the kitchen stone floor (not the best for Poor Clare bare feet) overlaid with linoleum, to covering our refectory tables with the left-over linoleum (Poor Clare form of tablecloths), to unravelling the mystery of how to assemble the shelves of the little metal stand brought all the way from Roswell in THE CRATE but unaccompanied by a how-to-do-it manual. There was the taking down of drapes and curtains and the lifting up in the chapel/choir by the same metal chains the same San Damiano crucifixes (miniatures of those in the big Roswell chapel/choir) that had sustained six homesick hearts in an earlier daughterhouse's beginning.

There was the discovery that an odd little bench could be persuaded that it was called to function as a book-rack on the organ, I personally having discovered that playing the organ accompaniments or ornamental music on a rack-less organ, while an obliging sister holds the accompaniment books with one hand and follows the liturgy from her Dutch missal clasped in her other hand, leaves definitely something to be desired. There was our first High Mass. And, yes, the Mass is a dramatic action. But this one had the added dramatic touch of the improvised "rack" plus the accompaniment book falling off the organ with a mighty crash. Our dear Dutch chaplain persevered through it all. Later we were to have an organ rack of less dramatic potentialities.

And there was the solemn erection of our chapter room altar (by which is meant: attaching it to the wall with stickers—it measured about twelve by five inches). It rose to hold a miniature crucifix from our first Roswell days and four-inch-high Roswell-homemade statues of St. Clare and St. Colette—and a relic of St. Francis. What more could be desired! Those were hard-working, happy days, not unmarked with a sudden surprise of tears for first one and then another at unanticipated moments when someone would suddenly remember that a parting lay proximately ahead. ". . . *There is nothing I am not prepared to undertake for love of you . . .*"

It was, of course, absolutely requisite that the community go to refectory from choir and back from refectory to choir in procession. This initially entailed our solemnly marching through the small boiler room and then through the kitchen where the cook paused in her final culinary preparations for dinner and stood at respectful attention as the procession of seven swept grandly by.

Almost equally requisite was having a refectory cart on which the server would steer the serving dishes toward the head table. And of like and absolute requirement was the head table itself, which gave cause for concern by reason of its considerably lacking the height maintained by the other two tables that had been given us. This concern was resolved by our hastily constructing leg-lifts for this table of humble height to allow it regal elevation such as would befit its station. The fact that the table acquired a habit of sliding off these lifts toward starboard side at given and not-given intervals during dinner did not disturb us. It needed only our hoisting it back into royal position after each of its listings.

A larger problem was—the cart. One simply must have a refectory cart if a foundation is to be rightly established. Wondrously, the same enchanted attic that had yielded us the linoleum revealed a cart. We felt established, once possessed of a refectory cart. And a remarkable one. For the wheels, doubtless in an earlier century round and capable of doing the usual business of wheels— rolling—had after what must have been a long career of faithful service in rolling, squared themselves off so as, presumably, to indicate that their rolling years were over. No matter. We had a refectory cart. So, the refectory server dutifully, and not without an appropriate sense of monastic usage, carried the cart over the threshold of the refectory, delivered its holdings to the head table, and then carried it back to the kitchen. Yes, we knew that we were established. And we felt so benign, having now a monastic procession, a head table for the refectory, and a refectory cart besides, that seven of us granted full pardon to our eighth member, who, in an excess of zeal for the laundry assigned to her as her special domain of community service, had carried off the remains of that prized roll of linoleum jubilantly discovered in the sprawling attic of our new home and covered the laundry floor with it. It was high thievery, she admitted, but justified, she assured us, by her zeal for the common good.

The days of prayer and song, of laughter and tears, of happily wearying hard work in organizing our temporary monastic home spun by. And it became evident that we were, all unintendedly, tracing large question marks in the minds of the dear folk who were helping us to subsist. These nuns never leave this mini-monastery of theirs. What are they so happy about? What is the mystery that invites young women to enclose their entire reach of physical living in a very small space? And they came to understand that the mystery is not a "what" but a "Who" and that in the enclosure of God's love is found the universal apostolate of the Poor Clares. It is not a matter of "leaving the world" but of stepping back from it so as to get a full view of "the miseries and hardships of the whole world", which our Poor Clare Constitutions tell us we are to hold to our hearts and enfold in our prayers and penances. It pertains to being so enclosed in Christ as to be able to embrace the whole world, of being somehow able to sweep a look of love over every aching heart and every agonizing need everywhere.

It was sufficient, that first evening of ours in Holland, for us to know that we were welcome, that one elderly man should bring us one small can of sardines. He had somehow brought all of Holland with him. And if we did not cross the ocean to proclaim from multiple rostrums resounding messages of scientific advance or to offer new theological findings or to proffer stunning plans and striking services to the multitude, hopefully we did bring to dear Holland the little "can of sardines" that is the gift of our lives of prayer and joyous penitence for the love of God and our adopted country.

"Nothing I am not prepared to undertake for love of you . . ." But then, on March 28, we found ourselves drawing back in failing courage from a "nothing" that included a definitive parting. Only then, he came, our spiritual father, His Eminence, Cardinal Mayer. He came from Rome and a so-exacting schedule to reinvigorate our flagging hearts and make all things possible *"for love of you, O God."*

With the privilege belonging to cardinals from the beginning, His Eminence came into the cloister and explored it thoroughly with us. He prayed part of the Divine Office with us. He offered Holy Mass in our miniature chapel the next morning. We renewed our holy vows in his hands, as in the very hands of our Mother the Church. And he sat in our little chapter room and spoke to us of the love of God, of sisterhood, of new beginnings, of painful sacrifice, and of loving willingness. There were many tears then, but sweeter ones, as we each of us felt herself being renewed.

Then that dreaded hour of parting came. Huddled together in the doorway of the cloister the six brave foundresses looked again so very small and so inexpressibly dear. I looked at them and thought: I cannot do it. They looked at me through tears that bespoke: We cannot do it. An ocean between us . . . this is too much. But then there was a blessing and a strong hand held out. And with the help of the great cardinal who had been summoned from his own country and community to serve the Church in Rome, we could do it.

The return flight across the Atlantic was a really fine-and-dandy Lenten penance. The plane was five and a half hours late in taking off, first delays for reasons not revealed to us, following delays because the plane's "warning horn" continued to sound its ominous tones when the plane prepared to take off. While fleets of mechanics came speeding out in little cars with flashing lights atop them, we consoled ourselves during the long wait by reflecting that it is considerably to be preferred that the plane resolve its crises on the ground rather than midway over the Atlantic Ocean. Yes, it was a long, weary flight (and, yes, of course, all this meant that we were to miss our connections in New York);

but, again, we had our Office to pray. When it all
seemed too long, too wearying, too unreal (how
did we ever get out of our cloister anyhow?), we
would pray another hour of the Office. Then we
could go on.

Again it was the Little Sisters of the Poor who
rescued two wilted wayfarers in the dark night and
bright lights of confusing (to cloistered folk, at any
rate) Kennedy airport, managed to get us wedged
onto another plane that followed by many hours
the original one we had missed, and gave the vibrant reality of their sisterly love to expunge from
our tired mental rosters something of the unreal-
ities of the return journey that had at that point
perdured for twenty hours and was to continue
for four more, as the plane came down in Wash-
ington to sit out a violent electrical storm before
it at length lifted again into the skies and at last
deposited two weary pilgrims on *terra firma*.

As we came in view of the monastery of our
youngest U.S. daughterhouse, we were resuscitated
from our exhaustion by the vision we saw. It was
now 12:15 A.M. and two of the sisters were waiting up to receive us. They had lighted the chapel,
so that we came toward a splendid "vision in the
night". The golden-lit spread of windows revealed
the cloister/chapel open grille before us. Throned
upon that green-golden expanse was the near life-

sized crucifix, our Lord's arms spread wide in redemptive love and in welcome for his weary pilgrims returned to this home from the new home abroad. We were swept into welcoming embraces. And then, for the other sisters whom we would greet the next morning, there sounded the rising bell for the midnight Office. The rhythm of our Poor Clare life went on. It goes on. And now it goes on anew in Holland, where six brave foundresses have vowed that *"There is nothing they are not prepared to undertake for love of you, O God"* and have brought their new country a little can of sardines. Their lives.

Chapter VII

Interlude

An Album of Moments

We have in these latter times taken up at community recreational gatherings a sharing of "moments", each Sister recalling for the others a memorable moment in her life that has inscribed an indelible truth upon her mind or indented an undebatable truth in her heart. In the large goings forth and abroad to make new foundations, there have occurred small, fleeting journeyings of the heart and of the understanding into new areas of love, new acres of, sometimes compassion, sometimes humility, sometimes flashes of faith gone beyond its ordinary earthly confinement. Or, such have occurred in the small interior goings forth and abroad into the fullness of a truth to which one has always assented but perhaps left largely unplumbed.

Swiftly they occur, these moments. Quickly they pass. But they leave blessedly deep grooves in the memory. They open the spirit upon meadows of larger understanding. In the very act of going forth either physically or spiritually—hopefully in a coupling of both—there have come lasting spiritual journeyings into new understanding. Before budding plans to go forth and abroad can lift us into the azure skies of the firmament or the opalescent skies of the interior understanding, there can be large ground flights into by-ways of the world's agony and despair. Or, again, along spreading runways of its hope.

I. Her Smile

Once when we stood in a crowd waiting to board a giant plane, I became aware of a gaze fixed piercingly on my person. My own eyes followed the radar of the spirit to find a woman seated on an airport "recliner" and staring at me with what was clearly neither mere curiosity nor, still less, only friendly interest. Her face was burdened with too many layers of make-up. Her clothing had its own obvious story to tell. Her male companion was readily identifiable as to his manner of living.

The woman looked so defiant, so hostile. I had no need to wonder why, when I felt I clearly knew why, knew that she somehow considered my religious garb, my veil, my appearance as indicating a way of life that brought down sharp censure on her way of life, perhaps a judgment and condemnation. A tidal wave of love and compassion broke over me. There was nothing to do, nothing to say. I could only smile at her with all the loving compassion that was flooding my heart for her in her unhappiness, which was far too real and too obvious to be concealed either under make-up or by resentment.

She stared. She blinked. I just went on smiling in unfaltering compassionate love. She bent forward a little. And then the disbelief on her painted face gradually relaxed. She smiled an uncertain, crooked but very real if tremulous little smile. Then my companion and I were hustled along in the boarding line and onto the plane. I do not know the woman's name. I have never seen her again. But we have met on a deep level. I know. It was a moment. And I pray for her each day of my life. We are friends.

II. God at Play

There is a very small plane that gets one into or out of Roswell to wherever one means to connect for farther going or from wherever one has come to this last and only available final flight-lap toward Roswell. And there are giant planes that have not yet discovered Roswell. These are three stories high, with stairways winding from one floor to another. Looking at such before boarding, one wonders how this dizzyingly large "hotel" can ever get off the earth and into the sky. Surely thousands of men together could not lift it one inch off the ground. It seems an overwhelming monument to the genius of men. Yet, to God, as he showed us, just a toy in his almighty hand.

For, on a particular Holland-bound midnight, in the impenetrable blackness of the glintless sky, the mysterious ocean surging unseen beneath us, we experienced such turbulence as never before on a giant plane. As though playing with his child's toy, God tossed the monstrous-large plane up and up again, then seemed to catch it in his divine hand only to turn it playfully from side to side. We felt that God was smiling on our small human achievements with benign amusement as he played with the three-storied plane while cards jumped out of the seat pockets and crew members clung to their seats. It was indeed a "moment".

As the mighty plane heaved and bent and rose and fell, it seemed clearly a time to pray. We began the rosary, starting with the fourth glorious mystery, Our Lady's Assumption into heaven, which seemed especially appropriate. We got to the fourth "Hail, Mary", and the turbulence immediately ceased. God's little toy then continued its giant course over the ocean with no other apparent comment from him, but leaving us a moment and a subsequent moment for recalling how God is definitely in charge of men's small affairs.

III. Celebration and Examination of Conscience

a. The attractive young mother was less embarrassed by the questions of her two small progeny than concerned to answer them with clear explanations.

We were on the airport shuttle bus bearing us from one plane to another as we returned from another "Forth and abroad". And a small girl and smaller boy were studying us with the piercingly inquiring gaze characteristic of children. Their voices were clear and resounding as, having studied us and our garb intently, they inquired of their mother, "Why do they dress like that?" We listened with interest as she fronted their questions with clear replies.

"You know how Mamma dresses up for a celebration, yes?" They did. They nodded with the certainty of children who keep their mental information files in good order. "You know how you

wear your best clothes when you go to a party?"
They did. They had firm and felicitous memories.
"Well, these two ladies celebrate Jesus every day.
And so they dress up for it. They are Sisters."

The children considered this, evidently judged
it a clear and convincing explanation, and gave us
the impression that they would consider celebrating on each and every day a capital idea. "Yes, they
celebrate Jesus every day. And that's why they dress
up."

It was perhaps the best explanation of the religious habit and, indeed, the consecrated virgin's
spousal love of Jesus that I have heard. The children understood it, in that way that children often
enough readily understand what some adults seem
not very easily to grasp or enduringly to penetrate.
The little girl put a thoughtful small finger in her
mouth. And smiled at us. It remains a moment to
treasure.

b. We were eating our lunch at the airport, waiting
for the plane to take us forth and abroad when we
heard a voice of such remarkable timbre, vigor and
volume as to make me think that Ethel Merman
was again among us.

"Look, George! Real nuns!"

We turned around, blushes warming our cheeks,
for "Ethel's" voice had quite penetrated the re-

cesses of the airport, establishing us as the focus of multiple gazings.

Real nuns. Well, it is what we want to be. It was a moment. It is unlikely that George's wife knew she was examining our consciences and calling us to time. We had better be what we want to be. And what we look like.

IV. *A Transoceanic Telephone Call*

It is a curious thing, meriting an in-depth consideration, that there is a notable lack of sweetness and kindness in those of our age who do not so much question ecclesiastical authority as deny and defy it. One searches fruitlessly for any modal gentility in the cacophonies produced by those who challenge with acerbity any firm magisterial stand or statement on truth at odds with their own distortions. The (hopefully) holy anger one can feel at attacks on the Pope in language that of itself expresses the mentality of the shouter must, in the end, resolve into a pity akin to indulgent mirth. For, on the level of intelligence alone, it does seem clear that most of us would need binoculars even to glimpse the top of this Supreme Pontiff's towering intellect. It is characteristic of truth that its real proponents are not habitually red in the face.

Word had gotten around before our going forth

and abroad to Holland that six Poor Clare nuns
plus myself and companion were coming to found
a new monastery. A humble beginning by some
assuredly humble little folk of no worldly distinc-
tion, definitely not a "power group" in the way that
term is ordinarily understood. It was more than
a surprise, then, when I received a transoceanic
telephone call from a secular newsman in Holland. Judging from his voice range and tonality,
I would have to say that, on that particular day at
least, he was not at his calmest. The quaver in his
voice when he demanded to know why we were
coming to the Netherlands was unmistakably not a
quaver of tenderness. I explained, happily enough,
that we were coming to live our cloistered life of
prayer and happy penance and thus to serve the
dear land about to receive us.

Calmo was not descriptive of his tonality when
he posed another question. "Are you trying to im-
pose Rome on us again?"

It was a moment. Of amazement that six little
folk should be held to be of such menacing power.
Of mirth that so small a contingent of love bearers
could be assessed as so large a threat. And of aching
compassion for warriors where there is no war.

V. The Angel

Each Sister in a Poor Clare monastery is gifted with a private cell in the dormitory as her own individual chamber in the house of the Lord. The word "cell", an ancient monastic term, derives from the Latin *cellula*, meaning "a very small room, usually that of a servant; a poor and humble little private apartment", descriptions dear to a daughter of St. Francis and St. Clare. The cell is a sister's place of rest, her private oratory, her little scriptorium for lectio and study, her sometimes place of work. Its poor and simple furnishings express her poor and simple life. The cell serves as a kind of little retreat house where a sister encounters and communes with the Divine Spouse, Jesus, in happy solitude and fruitful silence.

Poor Clare cells are furnished with the traditional bed of straw laid on boards set upon wooden trestles, a small stand or desk for ablutions and some work, a little wooden bench, and a cupboard for one's limited wardrobe. A simple image of our crucified Savior is placed on a small cloth laid upon a sister's pillow by day. It is a quaintly moving expression doubtful of ready understanding by those to whom the charism to penetrate the mystical reality has not been given. There is a spiritual reality likewise expressed by the bright sparseness of a Poor Clare's cell that includes upon its walls a crucifix before which the cell-dweller has accustomed herself more and more over the years to pray and from which she deepens her loving familiarity with Christ. There may also be two or three small unframed pictures of Our Lady or the saints, simply mounted. And a handcrafted holy water font. If there were a moving day to a different cell, it would not involve much. And when death comes, it would not need a loading platform for emptying the cell's contents.

Over each one's cell door hangs the identification sign of her who dwells therein. And after her solemn Profession, each nun hangs on a wall of her cell the crown of thorns she received at her consecration, that it may offer her a mutely eloquent daily reminder of the identification with Christ to which she is pledged and for which she is vowed to strive, and may likewise recall to her the enlivening reason for accepting the inevitable sufferings of her vowed life.

In a particular way, each sister's cell is her little garden enclosed where prayer blossoms and the presence of her Divine Spouse is fostered. It should be entirely predictable that as a sister grows older, the presence of God in her cell becomes ever more vibrant so that she returns to it as to a little castle of the King. So small by worldly standards, the cell will be as large as the heart of its occupant.

And that heart should become more and more aware with the passing years that there is another occupant of her cell, at least when she herself is present there. Does not each of us have a guardian angel whose definite presence is celebrated by the Church each year on the Feast of the Guardian Angels and whose reality also appears throughout Scripture? Yet, how possible it is to give full assent of mind to that presence with yet little practical advertence to the fact that it is no small thing to have an angel around—and in such close quarters as a Poor Clare's cell. But then there can come a moment when one is very consciously alerted to that presence.

Kneeling one night before the crucifix in the small cell apportioned to me, a sudden stab of knowledge rent my prayer. Yes, I have a guardian angel who never leaves me, will never desert me, who knows what I am about, and who does not merely observe me or keep a chart on my actions but encompasses me with God's own delegated love and desire for my holiness. Mentor, protector, constant companion, my guardian angel, ever present. And for a shining moment I knew it and experienced what I believe. There is an angel in this cell! In this small, poor cell of a small Poor Clare, there is an angel of God, a guardian angel. My angel. My guardian. It was indeed a moment. One always believes the truths of religion; but on occasion one knows them, too, when for a brief flash of light, faith becomes knowledge. The moment passes. Faith remains, but forever illumined by the moment.

As earlier noted, a cell is as large as the heart of its occupant. The moment made clear that one assuredly cannot offer hospitality to an angel in cramped quarters.

VI. *Processional*

Processions figure largely in Poor Clare life. We come from the choir to the refectory in procession. We return to the choir from the refectory in procession. We have May processions outdoors and Christmas carolling processions indoors, around the whole monastery complex. Processions we love for their own sake, for the joy of community marching along, praying or singing, and as rehearsal for the final procession from earth into eternity.

One evening I had been called from the choir and had to miss the procession. My business accomplished, I had just time to slip into a doorway on the route where the long double line of sisters was turning a corner. A warm sense of community washed over me. Pair after pair of bare feet marched past me. Happy small comments from the large Franciscan Crown rosary suspended from each nun's cord accompanied the singing voices. And a moment chimed in my heart: this is community, always going forward together, knowing where it is going and singing for the joy of going together.

It was well toward day's end, the day's work done, each sister's toil and prayers offered to God in a symphony of marching sisterhood. And in this symphony, each nun plays all the instruments. For is not each sister a sweeper, keeping the life of the community free of the ever-gathering dust and fuzzles of our human condition, and this by her own commitment to sisterly love and mercy? Is not each little poor one a bursar, careful that nothing is wasted and all opportunities for spiritual gain noted and applied? Do not the prayers and sacrifices of all the sisters reach out the messages of spiritual letters to all those asking our help? Must not each sister decorate our altars with her Eucharistic devotion? Shall not everyone nourish all her sisters with love and understanding, and this faithfully each and all the days? Must not the parched areas of life known by all at times be faithfully watered by the compassion of sisters? And shall not each sister's heart and

soul flower and blossom because she knows she is
loved by all the others? Is not each one called to
mend with understanding the torn and worn spiritual garments of her sisters? Does not each one,
beginning with the abbess and vicaress, share that
same grace of working that is to keep shining with
charity and garnished with sisterly affection the
whole spiritual compound, to tend all the spiritual
acres and girdle all the circling seasons with her
gift of herself?

The moment kept chiming its message: that
there are not greater and lesser works, no hier-
archies in that truest growth and service that all
share: the building and maintaining of a Franciscan
castle of love and peace for the Most High King.

Yes, the moment kept chiming its message: how,
each supplying for the other, the sisters go forward,
stumbling and rising, helped up and then helping
up, praying and pondering, sweeping and studying and cooking, tending and mending, crafting
and scrubbing, writing and repairing, singing and
chanting, playing the organ and plying the broom,
painting and weeding and all things other, in the
company of the sisters from whom God wonder-
fully creates out of human weakness a community
strong in purpose, fixed on one ideal, united in
him.

When eight of us set out for Holland, we numbered seven non-Dutch nuns and one Dutch nun. What a security! When our speech stuttered along its very meager Dutch vocabulary road and frequently suffered complete collapse, she could always be summoned to the rescue. She was a model of housewifery and got us all nicely organized in our little Elshout Village monastery in a minimum of time, needing only on our part a maximum of effort that her own manner of living always summoned forth. Capable of mind, efficient of procedure, she appeared to be undoubtedly the strongest physical specimen in our founding group. Sturdy of build, muscularly endowed, she was steward of a great store of energy and quite the valiant woman of the Scriptures who "puts her back into her work and shows how strong her arms can be" (Prov 31:17).

On one visitation of the young community, when I managed to take unto myself a share of the virus plaguing that part of Europe at the time, I had that best medication which is the absolute devotedness of spiritual daughters to a sick spiritual Mother. And this included the knowledgeable services of that dear Dutch spiritual daughter. There was, in this instance, also the notable devotedness of dedicated Dutch doctors, a pair of them. The first one came at 9:00 P.M. the initial night of my debacle. And I shall forever hold in prayerful and smiling memory not only his expert ministrations but also his uniquely solacing pronouncement: "You feel like you are going to die." Quite so. I did indeed, and given the dominance of the virus at that hour, the expectation was rather a pleasant one. Only the doctor added, "But it is not serious." At the time I had the temptation to think he had just made the mis-diagnosis of all time. However, time proved him right. And I returned to my prized share of domestic service, mine and the other sisters' always educated by our Dutch sister. Poignantly enough, her name was the same as mine. She was Sister Francis.

She was Sister Francis who some years before had crossed the ocean in reverse of our future crossing, coming to Roswell from Holland to become in time a full canonical member of our community. She had traveled alone. She knew no English when she came, but she learned it quickly enough in prayer, determination, and careful study, the study pertaining to the Scriptures, an English/Dutch grammar, and a book of fairy tales from which she would bring to recreation the fruits gathered from her studious pursuits of the storied travail of the beautiful princess harassed by the wicked stepmother.

This physically sturdy woman was the "never sick a day in my life" type. It continued so in Holland. Only in the Lent of 1993, her right arm got so lazy. So puzzling it was, for there was no pain, just limpness. No doubt a tired muscle. But, bewilderingly, her right leg soon followed suit. She could only drag her leg along the daily paths that it had always been her way to skim swiftly. It seemed that a doctor had better look into this. Maybe a full examination at the hospital was in order. Her muscles must need some professional toning up. Only it proved to be a matter, not of lapsing muscles, but of a tumor on the brain. A malignant tumor. A tumor not allowing of full removal without full disaster for the brain.

She was in shock, we were in shock at this diagnosis delivered to us by the surgeon on Holy Thursday. And the doctors were in a mind of marveling shock as Sister Francis, once having confronted and assessed her own situation, and this not without the mingling of her own human tears with ours, began to make businesslike inquiries of the doctors. How long? When the end is close, shall I be aware of it?

And so she returned to her spiritual and domestic labors in the monastery as best she could and with the diminishing that the summer months brought until she became entirely bedridden toward summer's end with her faculties failing as autumn came in. The last weeks she could not speak. At the near-end, she could not see. But she was aware that the sisters were at her side all day and all night, each of the days and each of the nights. She let them know when that moment that is the moment of all moments for each of us arrived for her. The whole little community was encircling her bedside. The chaplain had just been there. If only we could have the solace of knowing that she knew, knew that we were there.

And so she rendered the solace yearned for. She opened her eyes and slowly turned her gaze from one sister's face to another's. Her speechless "thank you!" filled the room, the monastery, surely the world and eternity, too. It was indeed a moment, a beautiful moment before flight. A moment to strengthen our life's journeying on.

It was September 21, 1993. And the moment of her enplaning for eternity keeps striking in the hearts of us all. The first fruits of our Holland foundation had been laid upon the altar of the Lord.

VIII. *The Conquering Crocus*

Rain is rare in Roswell. Snow yet more so. This particular winter had not been witness to such a rarity. Oh, so stony hard and dry the earth. We drove picks into it, toward early spring planting, at cost of all that our concerted muscular powers could muster. The boulder-dry earth seemed largely unimpressed by our continual watering.

How shall anything ever grow in our garden again, we wondered sadly. The hardness of the earth is master now over our best assaultive efforts. This is beyond our small human powers.

And then we saw it. A small golden crocus decided to announce the perseverance of spring over all we larger creatures call unassailable obstacles. Fragilely beautiful, endearingly tiny, the crocus shouldered its lovely way through the stony soil, pushing the heavy clods aside with such gentle determination as seemed to say: "Pardon me, but I have to reassure the children of men that spring is invincible, hope unconfoundable, God's love triumphant over impossibilities."

The hard earth broke and parted. And the little golden crocus, having made of the stony clods just a frame for its own lovely face, announced the power of beauty over the flintiest obstacles.

We stood around it, transfixed. It was a moment.

Chapter VIII

The Wedding Ring

"May I please ask you something?" the polite Dutch stewardess on the great plane bearing us to Holland inquired. She received a smiling affirmative from me, but her face remained grave, her gaze intent, her attention riveted on—as I realized with surprise—my hand. "It's that ring you are wearing . . ." Her voice trailed off. "I keep looking at it each time I come by." She knelt down in the aisle to get a better focus on my ring as I held out my hand to her. "It looks", she said, "like a wedding ring . . ." I told her that indeed it is, that it is the symbol of my life, of our vowed bridal lives.

Spouseship is not usually the subject of modern workshop gatherings. Nor of articles in current religious periodicals. Yet, exercising spouseship is the radical work of a vowed woman. It is the oldest and the newest truth to be pondered, and exercising it is the primary work of the heart, of the spirit. Every soul in every clime and every time is espoused to God by reason of its being created and called into being only out of the loving desire of his Will that it should be. Union with God is the only bond out of which life can issue. Life for the soul itself. Life to those in whom its own love begets and sustains and brings forth every newly unfolding love. Yet, there is a profoundly unique manifestation of spousal love that is a woman's whole returning of herself to God in religious vows.

In a play I was privileged to write on the life of great St. Teresa of Avila, I suggested St. Francis Borgia, her spiritual director, asking her what she thought it meant to be a woman. Teresa replies: "I think it means to love and to suffer." "And to be a nun—what is that?" St. Francis persists. Teresa knows: "I think it means to love and to suffer more."

There is much talk and many a brochure and quantities of volumes appearing in our time about the power that must be given or returned to women. They must be allowed full voice in the affairs of the Church, the government, the world. They have been deprived of power for too long. But the fact is that women are, simply by reason of being women, persons of massive power, and power beyond that of men.

If in marriage man provides the seed of life, it is only woman who can nurture the seed, enflesh it, bring it forth into flowering life. In all of this she exercises the power that is uniquely hers. And, as is true of all power, woman's singular power in being the life-bringer is realized in suffering. We tend, especially in our present time, to confuse power with dominance over others and over situations, whereas real power pertains to the understanding of what God has ordained that one should be. It is from love alone that feminine power derives. There is nothing a woman who knows she is loved cannot do. Even more importantly, there is nothing she will not do on behalf of her beloved. To exercise love's power is to have new vision, the new and profounder understanding that comes of looking out from the center of love.

This is assuredly not to say that women have never been used, exploited, put down. Who could disagree with the open testimony of every age, not exclusive of our supposedly enlightened own, that women have often been made merely the tools of men and the slaves of society. Yet, one need not search afar in history either to find men's dignity often dethroned by the wiles of women, while they are also frequently enabled to achieve greatness because of the unwavering faith of women. We need to agree on what we mean by power, hopefully to concur in concluding, if only from the clear evidence of history, that true power is that which endures and is triumphant in faith and lasting achievement rather than victorious in force and evanescent accomplishment.

Thus, one remembers the tragedy Delilah brought upon Samson, Cleopatra on Antony. Yet, one also recalls the mother in the Book of Maccabees, Mordecai's Esther, and how many others of such calibre. And one takes long thought of the *Virgo Potens*, Mother of God. If some in our age are particularly audible in demanding the liberation of women, there is perhaps need to look much more deeply into what liberation really means. From what? For what? It is necessary above all to take care that while justly seeking to liberate women from unjust oppression and inappreciative regard, we do not end by liberating women from their glory.

It is considered in many quarters today to be a great step forward into the emancipation of women that they have ready access to "remedies" against life. Has not woman always had the primary human control over beginning life? That she presently has readier means to terminate the life growing within her, has many eager to assist her in destroying her unique and tremendous power of nurturing maternal love, her own best glory, merely emphasizes the immensity of her power over life and death. The married (as also unmarried) woman has doubtless been often enough and oftener than enough maltreated, disdained, and left unaided in travail. Married or bondlessly allied or single, domestic or professional, she has frequently been disallowed to exercise her potential on the world scene, the political scene, even sometimes the ecclesial scene. But the real demise of power comes of not knowing what one's real power is. A woman's greatest and most perduring failure will be her losing the power to love. It is certainly not without significance that so many women presently pressing for power on the political, sociological, or ecclesial scene are appallingly unbeautiful in their unsmiling press for dominance. Contorted faces and clenched fists are particularly repellant in woman, who is gifted with unique powers to radiate love and extend healing hands.

Yes, much wrong has been perpetrated against women through all the centuries unto our own. Yet, also much wrong perpetrated *by* them even unto now, the greatest being the wrong against their own womanhood. In consideration of this latter, it appears not surprising that spousal love is not the watchword of the present hour nor brideship the banner of the day.

Once I was asked by an archbishop: "So, what is

wrong with women's religious life? Why are sisters pouring out of convents and monasteries? What went wrong?" It was not just a musing question, though I was aware that the prelate had indeed mused and sufferingly prayed over it, and at length. I said: "They have lost their sense of brideship. Or perhaps they never had it." We spoke of a meeting of men and women religious superiors where there had been, to an appalling degree, something resembling a real fight. And this about who was going to distribute Holy Communion at Mass. The women religious insisted on their "rights", although there were more than a hundred priests present. A kind of tragedy indeed that was, but hardly unpredictable. "Archbishop," I said, "when a religious woman loses her sense of brideship, she had better find it again else she will soon also lose her sense of womanhood. After that, she is not far from the peril of losing her faith."

The love of the religious woman for her crucified Christ has to be the center, the root, the meaning of her life. If it is not so, what reason would there be for not terminating one role of service in favor of something more personally inviting, more "modern", more novel, more self-pandering? And in the hours of that deep travail of the spirit, of the heart, that must come to all and from which women consecrated in religious life are assuredly not excluded or excused, what will keep the religious faithful in her consecration except a profound and tender love for a Divine Bridegroom. Hers. Religious life must be a life of service, true enough. Service to mankind, service to the Church, service to one's own community. But that is its expression, not its core. Its inmost core is spousal love for Christ. Not to hold Christ as the Bridegroom of the soul, and yes, of the heart, will inevitably leave a religious sooner or later with nothing but doing that tries to supply for the want of being and always tragically fails.

Once, when searching out the site for a new foundation, my companion and I gratefully accepted the overnight hospitality of some teaching religious. They were very hospitable and kind, but it was obvious that we were an anomaly to them. I felt for them, thinking it must surely seem to them, given their expressions, their apparel, and their interests, that we had fallen off another planet or were at least five hundred years behind the times. Yet, the next morning, when departing from them and thanking so very sincerely for their goodness in taking us in, I was totally unprepared for the "coordinator" of the group taking my hand, her eyes filled with tears, and asking: "Mother, you are so simple and so happy. Why aren't we?" Her question remains an ache in my heart for her and all her vast company of today, an ache in my prayer.

It is necessary that one be deeply rooted in one's own being, understanding that it has been struck off the Being of God, before one can come to recognize the beauty of submission in the spiritual and psychological preparation for understanding. As with faith itself, it cannot be a matter of "When I understand, then I shall believe", but, rather: "Unless you believe, you will never understand." Thus, unless a woman has come humbly to accept the responsibility of her power, she cannot exercise the full spiritual mechanics of love and suffering that are rooted in her nature and that provide the greatest dynamism ever known or yet to be known to the world.

Women, long or presently downtrodden, crying out for respect and recognition, are already in that very action power figures in the most profound sense. Power is to be acknowledged not only in vindication of rights and assumption of certain primacies, desirable and praiseworthy as such may be, but also and more radically in each new expression of the triumph of love and suffering over wrong and even evil. The all-powerful God was all-triumphant on the Cross. One needs to search out the meaning of things.

Who are the great power figures in the Passion of Christ? The period of Jesus' earthly life was hardly one offering historical verification of women leading nations or holding high offices in government. Yet then, as now, or in that later century when a young peasant girl was to lead all the French forces to victory and make possible the crowning of the Dauphin at Rheims, or again when a young Sienese woman was to prevail upon the Pope to betake himself back to his proper home and throne in Rome when no male forces had been able either to persuade or to force him in that direction, women have been power figures.

Indeed, woman must exercise her powers, but she needs to know what they are. She has the right and the duty of her womanhood to discover and point out beauty, to confess the truth about herself, first to herself and then to all, to persevere in goodness under whatever travail. The ancient triad of beauty, truth, and goodness is primarily entrusted to woman. And there is her fashioning by God himself for suffering. Tears are her best battle cry. Nor is that a play on words.

We see the love-companies of women following after Jesus and, as the Scriptures so engagingly put it, "looking after his needs" (Mk 15:41). We find them fearlessly stepping out of the shouting and menacing crowd to make their way through the bands of soldiers and gather around a pain-staggering Jesus. No one, it appears, dared to halt them. Or, evidently, even thought of it. And to do what? Shout out protest? Shriek for justice? No, just to weep for the One they loved. They risked their lives and the lives of the infants on their arms just to make clear to Jesus that they loved him more than their lives. There was Veronica, who, whether by historical fact or by force of dramatic fable, fearlessly manifested a love-power so great that she could simply part the soldiers and ruffians surrounding Jesus on his Way of the Cross and make her way through to offer solace to him whom she loved more deeply than life itself. Again —to do what? Utter an impassioned and wholly deserved condemnation of his murderers? No, just to wipe the sweat and blood from his face. Under the Cross, man was outnumbered by woman. Two feminine power figures stood there with strength of love so great that no soldier dared drag or even wave them away. Two women. The Immaculate Mother of God and a converted woman of the streets.

Nowhere in the Scripture accounts of the Passion do we find a woman in least way party to the incomparable crime of man's murdering God. They were the power group, the scriptural women of the Passion, just following Jesus, looking after his needs.

What are the particular needs of Christ and his beleaguered Church of our day? Are they not the unshakable loyalty that pertains so peculiarly to woman and voices that are raised in a healing of love rather than a rending violence? Again, all this is by no means to say that women in our day have not been ignored, used, and abused in how many instances. Yet, it does give pause to obeserve some women apparently unable to articulate their cause with the dignity that woundedness itself should be able to summon forth (we observe Christ in his Passion), but resorting to snatching microphones and shouting others down. Misuse or abuse of power invariably pertains to stridor, from whichever side the misuse and abuse may issue. Somewhere in the shouting crowds and the volcanic anger there has been a radical destruction of woman's power to forgive and go positively forward.

Thus, if women's rights have often enough been denied, withheld, struck down, one cannot express a proper indignation or take right measures of vindication unless one understands what lies at the deepest level of exercising power. What has become of spousal love, the most powerful force given to women in whatever vocation in life? Where is the all-forgiving strength of women that echoes Christ's prayer upon the Cross: "Father, forgive them. They do not know what they are doing" (Lk 23:34).

As Hosea did not just take back Gomer, his faithless wife, but bought her back (Hos 3:2), so, too, contrariwise, must the faithful Gomers give of the very substance of their hearts to buy back errant Hoseas. Nor does errancy pertain alone to the sphere of moral integrity in conjugal love. Wanderings off the path of reverence, away from the enhancing of the liturgy that comes of preserving its radical beauty and meaning in a setting of blossoming beauty and compelling dignity, these also pertain to errancy.

One hardly need search very widely to assemble a folio of evidence that the setting of the Mass and the sacramental liturgy have often enough and in many places been seduced by rough, unintelligent, unspiritual expressions into becoming a distasteful exhibitionism having little to do with divine mysteries and worship. It could perhaps well be very different if women in general were pressing forward to break the alabaster vases of their specific gifts for bringing and sustaining loveliness, and for nurturing beauty and dignity, instead of pressing toward the pulpit and the altar, if they were favoring and raising a cry for the return of reverence over a cry for their "ecclesial rights".

And what, really, are a woman's specific ecclesial rights? Do they not derive from the *Mater Ecclesiæ* and *Mater Dei* who gathered the young Church about her after the crucifixion, strengthened the first priests of Christ her Son with the power of her persevering womanliness, and "held it all together"? It is particularly woman's role in any life situation to "hold it all together". She is fashioned for bearing and holding and protecting life whether on the natural or supernatural level. Hers to bring grace and dignity to life in a manner specific to herself. If our Mother the Church has in our time been in many ways deprived of the expressions of her maternal spiritual love and of her grace and beauty, is it not a verifiable explanation that many women have joined the forces of deprivation?

We must pay out our radical coins of love and suffering for anything worthwhile ever to be achieved, as is made clear in the life of Christ. Thus, when the religious woman vows obedience, chastity, poverty, she is not making herself partner to deprivation but in a most wonderful way exercising her right to submit in order to hold high command of her will, her right to do without in order to exercise the highest ownership which is to have disowned proprietorship, her right to forego the love of a man for the love of God.

St. Clare summed up all three vows taken by

religious in a brief and most inviting admonition: "As a poor virgin, cling to the poor Christ." And, then, for her own daughters, there was to be a fourth vow: enclosure. As she saw all the vows as pertaining to the freedom she penetrated by that poetry of the heart that is the birthright of woman if not necessarily her copyright, so she understood a call to the cloister to be an invitation to take up residence in the King's rooms.

Enclosure is a mystery to many. Why must one be enclosed in a restricted confine? Worse, or at least more baffling still, is the Church's laying down some very clear legislation about it. Are not religious women who are called to be contemplatives suffering assault on their freedom by being obliged to remain in the cloister in order to be cloistered nuns? It needs to be understood that a call to the cloister is just that—a call, an invitation. And this from the Most High King. To respond to such an invitation is hardly to curb one's power.

"The King has brought me into his rooms" (Song 1:4). A vocation to the cloister is just as simple and yet as incredible, as exquisite, and still as demanding as that. Through multiple centuries, flurries have arisen, debates have been compounded, and "liberation movements" inaugurated against the supposed strictures of cloister that curtail the freedom of religious women called to the contemplative life. It is as though enclosure were the price one had to pay for being a vowed contemplative.

Present (though by no means new) debate about the Church's legislation regarding enclosed nuns seems to generate only multiplying confusions and even sometimes a notable emotional heat. But how could it be otherwise when those concerned are not speaking the same language, when there is a confusion of tongues inevitably making for further confusion of thought.

The hall down which the contemplative is called to be brought into the King's rooms is, like all halls, by nature and by function, an avenue. It leads somewhere. It connects divergent expressions of function and gathers them into unity. This is most evident in that spiritual hall down which one called to the cloister moves in order to answer the King's invitation to come into his rooms. It is not a dead-end hall. Rather, it gives off into mysteriously multiplying rooms of self-giving. If enclosure is rightly understood and ever-increasingly cherished, it will invite, even lovingly direct, its dwellers to the profoundest self-donation in spousal love. The King's rooms stand revealed as threatening housing for those who wish to reserve anything of themselves for themselves or to set up independent duchies for specific avocations, however worthy these might well be for those called to exercise them.

A contemplative summoned down that most intimate hall of the King which is the enclosure quickly enough and increasingly with the years of her occupancy discovers how the divine hall of her living winds down the avenue of the whole universe and opens upon the rooms of every need and suffering of the entire world that can be fully visited, explored, and served only by a complete deliverance of one's self in that contemplative prayer and penitence of heart and modality of life that penetrate the otherwise inaccessible, serving those aching needs of a tortured and lonely world in hidden giving of self.

That this royal hall into the King's dwelling gives on to all the rooms of mankind is stated in the Constitutions of the Poor Clares in that same matter-of-fact way that is characteristic of the Scriptures. Those called down the hall of the King are summoned "to share in the most universal way the hardships, miseries and hopes of all mankind" (art. 2, no. 1). King's hall gives on myriad interior rooms of those cosmic realities. And while we greatly admire those who have received from God a wondrous call to glorify him and to serve and heal, teach and counsel portions of mankind through a specific service to a particular sector of the realm, those who are called to the cloister must understand that their specificity of service pertains not to particular action but to the universality of their oblation. "Pray, therefore, the Lord of the harvest that he send forth laborers into his harvest" (Mt 9:38), directed that very Lord of the harvest, making it clear that need is served primarily by prayer.

And so some are summoned over the variant vineyards of the kingdom. But others are called to come into the King's rooms and remain there. All the called are called not only to serve the "others" of the kingdom but to serve one another. This is best achieved by a clarity about one's own call and a respect for the life's linguistics of those whose lives are all destined to proclaim God, but not in the same dialect.

If this is not understood, we shall open ourselves to the evident danger of forsaking the beauty, the truth, and the goodness of spiritual intramurals for the forensics of non-understanding. And, unfortunately, these forensics, as is readily observable all around us, can become polemics. For one who is called into the King's hall of the enclosure, it is not a case of being herded in but precisely of being summoned. If the Church through all the centuries has provided and does still provide in love for the spiritual maintenance of the King's rooms of the cloister, the contemplative does not think of ecclesiastical legislation as restrictive but as liberty, since love is always liberating and perhaps supremely so when it enfolds the beloved in its arms. This is how the cloistered nun must understand the jealous vigilance of the Church for her contemplatives through all the centuries. This is how she allows herself that most intimate security which is to be held in the embrace of the one who loves her.

What, then, is "ecclesiastical legislation" regarding papal enclosure? It is precisely the arms of the Church cherishing her contemplatives. And thus, if an enclosed nun is encouraged by some to rebel at "strictures", she will let her smiling silence itself best explain that she is not incarcerated but cherished. For her, "legislation" pertains to that realization that the arms of the Church are around her. And she rejoices, as any normal woman rejoices to be held in loving arms. She has penetrated beneath the level of "legislation" as restrictive or prohibitive to the understanding of how love of its nature seeks to safeguard the beloved. Thus her understanding of ecclesiastical legislation on her cloistered life is expressed in the cry of the psalmist: "How I love your law, O Lord!" (Ps 119). This, then, is the demanding and gloriously rewarding *modus vivendi* of those called into the King's hidden rooms.

If it has been well said that there is no lie like a half-truth, we may add that there is no confusion like the splintering and fragmenting of truth. The mind hungers for the fullness of truth that will be realized entirely only in eternity, when at last the soul has been completely freed of its earthly limitations. Yet, even when not yet emancipated from the shackles of earth, it is that fullness of truth in the measure possible to human existence that the soul and, yes, the mind ache to possess.

This pure longing is too often blurred in its vision by particles of truth become dissociated from one another so as to present the mind with a dust storm rather than an unclouded sweep of vision. In the King's rooms the cloistered contemplative is obliged to encounter truth in all its demanding starkness, which alone makes for liberating understanding. Truth can be well served by scholarship, but it is never the result or reward of scholarship alone, and still less the guaranteed result of prolific workshops that are sometimes observably superficial, however well-intentioned.

"A little learning is a dangerous thing", remarked Alexander Pope. The little fragmented "truth" of a shibboleth, a slogan, the day's placard, pertains to confusion, not to understanding. For the contemplative, truth is revealed in the King's rooms of prayer. It comes of confrontation of one's self under the King's gaze, at once devastating and healing. Devastating in its sweeping away of particled truths and the illusions they beget, healing in its revelation of the King who said of himself: "I AM the truth" (Jn 14:6).

It is essential that the cloistered contemplative give assent to the whole truth about herself and her way of life, with its need of a royal ecclesial guard to stand love-watch over it. In the soul's nudity before God, the King, is found room for the fullness of truth about cloistered contemplative life that is a glory to be humbly and sufferingly borne and, in a degree, to be achieved. Has not everyone experienced at some time the understanding that springs up in oneself at encountering the sheer truth of another person? It needs not so much to be taught, much less explained, as just to be seen. Once when Cardinal Mayer walked into our chapter room, a young nun who had never seen him before said afterward: "I felt like truth had walked into the room."

The King's room of truth needs safeguarding. It is not at multiple outside meetings and gatherings and discussions, but in the interior meeting with herself before God in the all-demanding workshop of prayer, in the gathering together in God of her scattered being and in profound interior (and exterior also) silence of her soul, that the contemplative discovers truth. It is in contemplation that the contemplative comes up against the both dev-

astating and exhilarating, demanding and rewarding fullness of truth.

Then there is the encounter with beauty in the
King's rooms, beauty not much evident in many of
the vigorous chafings against that protective love of
the Church for her cloistered contemplatives. We
do protect what we hold precious. That agreed, it
seems more than strange that there should be sometimes vigorous protest against protection. Could it
be that we are no longer holding cloister precious?
Is woman's gift of suffering to be squandered where
there is cause here rather for wondrous rejoicing?

Cloistered contemplative life has sometimes been
reduced to a dreariness of imposed routine where
it should have been elevated to the heady exhila-
ration of discovery. It is necessary that cloister be
held in the hands of the heart like a jewel, turning
facet after facet in the sun of the King's love. The
beauty of the contemplative life is poorly served
by devices, but it is revealed in the depths of the
life itself. And what is made ever more manifest
in the depths will become increasingly evident on
the delightful upper levels of the small everyday
experiences.

As I sit here in the sunlight of a tenderly waning
spring afternoon, I look up to see the dishtowels
drying on the clotheslines. We are (for contempla-

tive nuns) a large community. There are lots of dinner dishes, lots of dishtowels to perform their postprandial work. They are so beautiful, there in the breeze, those dishtowels, billowing with ballerina grace and reaching out in arabesques when the breeze gives larger exhalations. They have their own workshop to offer about the grace of simple things and the importance of respecting them. There is, after all, no valid excuse for hanging dishtowels in graceless bunches. But these things that belong to prayer, to awareness of God and community, to delighting in all beauty even in its simplest expression, are not usually emphasized at meetings on the liberation of cloistered nuns but only in the King's rooms where the smallest sign of beauty immediately alerts the soul to prayer and somehow mystically radiates out to an often graceless world the beauty that lurks in all created things.

Right now, though, I am distracted from the dancing dishtowels that teach me, in their own fashion, how to rejoice in the King and his creation. For a very small bird is climbing a very large tree just in front of me, his tiny body achieving effortless parallel to the tree. Amazing. Not one of us could climb that tree in such parallel with such trusting assurance. How beautiful that God could create this small creature with its easy grace beyond any such attempted feat of ours. One has to pray, to praise God, to delight in it all. Right in the King's room from which the contemplative's prayer sends out an urgent alert to all the wounded and weary world to be on watch for God's daily workshop in the mysterious assuaging of the world's pain by beauty's enduring testimony to him and the world to come. Birdsong still outlasts the longest war. And full donation of self in love the most perduring polemics.

Thus did stigmatized St. Francis of Assisi, hobbling on nail-riven feet, sing out the miracle of beauty's healing. Thus must the enclosed contemplative sing out from the King's room what she can learn only there. Mother Teresa of Calcutta presents a convincing argument in favor of allowing children to be born when she inquires how the sick can get well if there are no children to smile at them. How shall a world groaning under the weight of dissension and hatred "get well" without the ministry of that hope in God which is served by beauty discovered in the intimacy of total self-giving? Or if those appointed to send out the message of hope from the King's room become themselves dissenters? Or if they initiate an ersatz suffering that gnaws at the vitals of real love? Pope John XXIII once remarked that "nothing is so wasted as suffering." A woman must not waste her best talent.

And then there is the crown of the ageless triad: goodness holding sceptre upon truth and beauty. Here is the sublime industry exercised in the King's room to which the enclosed contemplative nun has been called: the maintaining of the truth that enclosure is not a bondage but a precious freedom for the spirit to roam the acres of God according as the body rests content in his room under love-guard of the Church. The proclamation of the beauty of God experienced in spousal love in that cleft of the rock that is the Heart of the King must go out to the ends of the world. And the urgent message of God's goodness to the straining battalions of the world groaning under the weight of evil and hatred and unending wars.

Surely it is not a debatable good to have been called into the King's rooms of enclosure, nor a dubious good that Holy Church sets the royal guard of her solicitous love at the entrance.

For what the enclosure encloses is a woman in love. She is exercising the power of woman in a unique and wondrous way, all things made possible by reason of her vowed love relationship to her Lord and King. Consecrated spousal love pertains to the core of the heart, and it ofttimes makes suffering demands, demands in their turn made desirable just because of love. It is a blessed circle and expressed in the ring circling the Poor Clare's finger. The ring bears the outline of a heart. And of a cross. The vowed contemplative has assumed a power over the world's agony and need by reason of being espoused to the all-powerful King. She has agreed to exercise on behalf of the whole world's pain a woman's power to suffer and to heal. Were the cloistered religious life only a matter of pious routine, leisurely prayer, and a lifelong leave of absence from the travail of the rest of the world, it would be, not just reprehensible in the eyes of suffering mankind, but an affront upon a nun's own being. But not for long. For she would leave the King's rooms, never having really discovered them to be that.

A few years ago, we were gifted with the penance of yet another nationwide questionnaire. We bore the weight of its multiple pages to an evening recreation. And we laughed and laughed. Not at the questionnaire, and still less at its authors, but just at the ridiculousness that has to issue forth when, like Atlas, one holds the world upon one's shoulder in spherical investigations of same, only like him (as Sister Madeleva has remarked in one of her poems) to "miss the point entirely of the grand Deific theme". The questionnaire was concerned with our scholastic degrees. How many? Please note the number with Ph.D.s. "Let's all just sign 'x' and explain that we have not yet learned to read and write", suggested one young minstrel. "We could tell them that 'Mother always signs documents and questionnaires for us, as we can't write.' " This from another young jester. There were many questions about our "jobs". Some wanted to write a long job description about the care and nurturing of squash and tomatoes, our best garden crops, with warnings about muscle protest that one must learn to ignore in favor of loftier concerns. The questionnaire was concerned about difficulties in our jobs, about our talents being non-used. A few whom all lovingly but firmly recognize as persons to be kept out of the kitchen and away from the stove at all cost protested that they have never been allowed to exploit their talents, even as a new recreational huzzah of favor toward continuing that course of action arose.

It went on and on. But then, suddenly, we came upon the questions, "Are you planning to leave your community soon?" and "When you leave your community, what do you plan to do? What job do you want?" And all the laughter died as on a strike of lightning. A darkness settled upon the room. In one fell moment, all understood that there really were persons in religious life who thought and apparently lived in a "job domain". Lifelong consecration to Christ in religious vows? Spouseship with the King? Seemingly these were unconsidered because, perhaps, never understood or even encountered. A deep shared sadness came upon us in the sudden silence. And then a sense of gratitude that in community one shares all things with the others, including sadness.

It is only the love of a Divine Bridegroom that can explain a nun's fidelity unto death and into eternity. Spouseship is, in the end, the most beautiful expression of power, the unleashing of such love and willingness to suffer the lot of the Bridegroom as alone makes for the triumph of womanhood in whatever vocation.

At the ceremony of a Poor Clare's solemn Profession, when a young nun tosses her life like a song into the Heart of Christ as alms for all in his kingdom, a ring is placed upon her finger. And then a crown of thorns upon her head. That is the proper order of things, for it is only love that makes bearing the reality of thorns possible. So, there it is again: a woman exercising woman's great power to love and to suffer for God and all his people. The newly ringed and crowned young nun who has pronounced her vows with her hands placed in those of the abbess while the bishop looks on

in witness lifts her gaze to the eyes of her abbess.
It is a moment that never fades.

"It looks like a wedding ring", the stewardess
said. It is.